South Asian Creative and Cultural Industries

It is widely acknowledged that creativity is emerging as one of the most important sources of economic growth. This book investigates the varied forms of the creative and cultural industries including the arts, culture, film, design and other related fields.

In this book, the chapters showcase new research insights into the recent growth of the creative and cultural industries, which can be located across the intersection of the arts and humanities, business studies and social science disciplines. The contributors provide rich empirical insights about the creative and cultural industries of and connected with South Asia, both from its diasporas and around the world. This includes a variety of examples of creativity from the Bollywood film industry, to the growth of the creative sector in countries like the UK, India and Bangladesh, making the book an engaging read for anyone who is interested to learn more.

Using contemporary and original cases from South Asia and its diasporas, *South Asian Creative and Cultural Industries* offers new research perspectives on a growing and important region of the world. This book was originally published as a special issue of the *South Asian Popular Culture* journal.

Khaleel Malik is Senior Lecturer at Alliance Manchester Business School/Manchester Institute of Innovation Research in the University of Manchester, UK. He has researched and published many articles in international journals mainly focusing on innovation management and innovation policy. He is also the Book Review Editor of the journal *R&D Management*.

Rajinder Dudrah is Professor of Cultural Studies and Creative Industries in the School of Media, Birmingham City University, UK. He has researched and published widely across film, media and cultural studies. He has authored and co-edited numerous books, including *Bollywood Travels: Culture, Diaspora and Border Crossings in Popular Hindi Cinema* (Routledge). He is also the founding co-editor of the journal *South Asian Popular Culture*.

South Asian Creative and Cultural Industries

Edited by
Khaleel Malik and Rajinder Dudrah

LONDON AND NEW YORK

First published in paperback 2024

First published 2020
by Routledge
4 Park Square, Milton Park, Abingdon, Oxon OX14 4RN

and by Routledge
605 Third Avenue, New York, NY 10158

Routledge is an imprint of the Taylor & Francis Group, an informa business

© 2020, 2024 Taylor & Francis

All rights reserved. No part of this book may be reprinted or reproduced or utilised in any form or by any electronic, mechanical, or other means, now known or hereafter invented, including photocopying and recording, or in any information storage or retrieval system, without permission in writing from the publishers.

Trademark notice: Product or corporate names may be trademarks or registered trademarks, and are used only for identification and explanation without intent to infringe.

Publisher's Note
The publisher has gone to great lengths to ensure the quality of this reprint but points out that some imperfections in the original copies may be apparent.

Disclaimer
Every effort has been made to contact copyright holders for their permission to reprint material in this book. The publishers would be grateful to hear from any copyright holder who is not here acknowledged and will undertake to rectify any errors or omissions in future editions of this book.

British Library Cataloguing in Publication Data
A catalogue record for this book is available from the British Library

ISBN: 978-0-367-43756-5 (hbk)
ISBN: 978-1-03-283901-1 (pbk)
ISBN: 978-1-00-300800-2 (ebk)

DOI: 10.4324/9781003008002

Typeset in MinionPro
by Deanta Global Publishing Services, Chennai, India

Contents

	Citation Information	vii
	Notes on Contributors	ix
1.	South Asian creative and cultural industries: Introduction *Khaleel Malik and Rajinder Dudrah*	1
2.	Beyond the creative class, mapping the collaborative economy of Bangladeshi creative industries: Case study of *Oitij-jo* *Lipi Begum and Maher Anjum*	5
3.	What 'value' South Asian arts in Britain? *Jasjit Singh*	22
4.	The production of *Ek Tha Tiger*: A marriage of convenience between Bollywood and the Irish film and tourist industries *Giovanna Rampazzo*	33
5.	'New Bollywood' and the emergence of a 'Production House' culture *Amrita Goswami*	51
6.	Optimize the contribution of design to innovation performance in Indian SMEs – what roles for culture, tradition, policy and skills? *Simon Bolton, Lawrence Green and Bhavin Kothari*	64
7.	Envisioning the future: Financialization and the Indian entertainment industry reports *Nitin Govil*	83
8.	Bahrisons New Delhi: Commerce and creativity in Khan Market *Emma Varughese*	99

9. Impacts of funding in digitising the Bangladesh film industry:
   Challenges ahead   105
   Muhammad Shajjad Ahsan

10. Creative enterprise from the medieval to the modern period:
    Alternative perspectives   113
    Catherine Casson

    Index   119

Citation Information

The chapters in this book were originally published in the journal *South Asian Popular Culture*, volume 14, issue 3 (October 2016). When citing this material, please use the original page numbering for each article, as follows:

Chapter 1

South Asian creative and cultural industries: Introduction
Khaleel Malik and Rajinder Dudrah
South Asian Popular Culture, volume 14, issue 3 (October 2016) pp. 133–136

Chapter 2

Beyond the creative class, mapping the collaborative economy of Bangladeshi creative industries: Case study of Oitij-jo
Lipi Begum and Maher Anjum
South Asian Popular Culture, volume 14, issue 3 (October 2016) pp. 137–153

Chapter 3

What 'value' South Asian arts in Britain?
Jasjit Singh
South Asian Popular Culture, volume 14, issue 3 (October 2016) pp. 155–165

Chapter 4

The production of Ek Tha Tiger: *A marriage of convenience between Bollywood and the Irish film and tourist industries*
Giovanna Rampazzo
South Asian Popular Culture, volume 14, issue 3 (October 2016) pp. 167–184

Chapter 5

'New Bollywood' and the emergence of a 'Production House' culture
Amrita Goswami
South Asian Popular Culture, volume 14, issue 3 (October 2016) pp. 185–197

Chapter 6

Optimize the contribution of design to innovation performance in Indian SMEs – what roles for culture, tradition, policy and skills?
Simon Bolton, Lawrence Green and Bhavin Kothari
South Asian Popular Culture, volume 14, issue 3 (October 2016) pp. 199–217

Chapter 7

Envisioning the future: Financialization and the Indian entertainment industry reports
Nitin Govil
South Asian Popular Culture, volume 14, issue 3 (October 2016) pp. 219–234

Chapter 8

Bahrisons New Delhi: Commerce and creativity in Khan Market
Emma Varughese
South Asian Popular Culture, volume 14, issue 3 (October 2016) pp. 235–240

Chapter 9

Impacts of funding in digitising the Bangladesh film industry: Challenges ahead
Muhammad Shajjad Ahsan
South Asian Popular Culture, volume 14, issue 3 (October 2016) pp. 241–248

Chapter 10

Creative enterprise from the medieval to the modern period: Alternative perspectives.
Catherine Casson
South Asian Popular Culture, volume 14, issue 3 (October 2016) pp. 249–254

For any permission-related enquiries please visit:
http://www.tandfonline.com/page/help/permissions

Notes on Contributors

Muhammad Shajjad Ahsan is Professor in the Department of Drama and Dramatics, Jahangirnagar University, Bangladesh.

Maher Anjum believes in connecting all the dots to provide sustainable long-term solutions that look after people, planet and profits. Maher has successfully managed across various sectors including the creative industries.

Lipi Begum is Senior Marketing and Management Lecturer at University of Wales Trinity Saint David, London Campus, UK.

Simon Bolton is Chair of Innovation and Associate Dean in Employability and Enterprise, Faculty of Arts and Science at Edge Hill University, UK.

Catherine Casson is Lecturer in Enterprise in the Innovation Management and Policy Division of Alliance Manchester Business School at the University of Manchester, UK.

Rajinder Dudrah is Professor of Cultural Studies and Creative Industries in the School of Media, Birmingham City University, UK. He has researched and published widely across film, media and cultural studies.

Amrita Goswami is a PhD student in the department of Cinema Studies, School of Arts and Aesthetics, Jawaharlal Nehru University, New Delhi.

Nitin Govil is Associate Professor of Cinema and Media Studies in the School of Cinematic Arts at the University of Southern California, US.

Lawrence Green is Senior Lecturer in the Department of Strategy, Enterprise and Sustainability, Manchester Metropolitan University, UK.

Bhavin Kothari is Associate Senior Faculty within the Strategic Design Management discipline at the National Institute of Design, India.

Khaleel Malik is Senior Lecturer at Alliance Manchester Business School/*Manchester Institute of Innovation Research* in the University of Manchester, UK.

Giovanna Rampazzo completed her PhD at the Centre for Transcultural Research and Media Practice, Dublin Institute of Technology, Ireland.

Jasjit Singh is Research Fellow at the University of Leeds (UK) based in the School of Philosophy, Religion and the History of Science.

Emma Varughese is an Independent Scholar and a Senior Fellow at Manipal Centre for Humanities, India.

South Asian creative and cultural industries: Introduction

Khaleel Malik and Rajinder Dudrah

Introduction

This special issue brings together an exciting set of articles on the theme of 'South Asian Creative and Cultural Industries'. We present new work on and about the creative and cultural industries of, related to, and connected with South Asia, both from across its diasporas and from around the world. The papers selected showcase interesting and informative research contributions that one can locate across the intersection of the arts and humanities, business studies and social science disciplines. In many parts of the world the creative and cultural industries are contributing to the making of place and space in terms of urban regeneration, which include novel ways of managing work–life relationships, particularly as people work and consume the products of these industries in different ways. As such popular cultures are often formed and shaped anew in and through these industries and their cultural practices. The value of creative and cultural industries in some developing economies of South Asia is often linked to their ability to: stimulate cultural and social development; and provide an economic tool for growth and development based on the potential to create employment, generate income, earn export revenues and alleviate poverty (UNCTAD 123–131).

Many people acknowledge that creativity is emerging as one of the most important sources of economic growth. Hence investing in the creative and cultural industries should entail more than just pumping up Research and Development spending or improving Education, though both are important to these industries. It requires increasing investment in the varied forms of creativity such as the arts, culture, music, design and other related fields, because all are linked and flourish together. As stated by Florida (320), this also means investing in the related infrastructure and communities that attract creative people from around the world and that broadly stimulate creativity. Here, it is also worthwhile mentioning that one of the major difficulties encountered by creative and cultural industries is the challenge of establishing and sustaining a business given that these industries often have relatively low level of firms that eventually grow and assume dominant roles in relevant markets (Cox 10–15). Despite these difficulties, mangers working in the creative and cultural industries often demonstrate an entrepreneurial flair. Swedberg (249) attributes this to the leadership qualities of these entrepreneurs as being dynamic, active and energetic leaders. They must also be ready to identify and grasp market opportunities, undertake risks and try out new combinations. This requires them to be creative in unique and sometimes unexpected ways (Aggestam 30–53), which is a key feature found in many of the articles presented in this special issue.

Contributions

The first two articles of this special issue examine how South Asian arts and culture have developed in the UK recently, where arts and culture transcends across many areas including visual arts, theatre, museums, music and storytelling. Utilising infographics and netnographic interviews, Lipi Begum and Maher Anjum's paper 'Beyond the Creative Class, Mapping the Collaborative Economy of Bangladeshi Creative Industries: Case study of *Oitij-jo*' documents how the British Bangladeshi diaspora in the UK have been collaborating to contribute to the growth of the creative sector in the UK and Bangladesh. They show how a not-for-profit open platform like *Oitij-jo* can enhance a wealth of networks that are necessary for nurturing entrepreneurship and growth. *Oitij-jo* can be summarised as a heritage that is learning from and looking at the past, for the present. It started out with the vision to present creative excellence and achievement of Bengali traditions in the arts and crafts. This paper helps us to appreciate that 'creatives' in the *Oitij-jo* context include those who were directly working as creative practitioners such as musicians, dancers, filmmakers, photographers, writers and curators. Creatives working with some non-creatives (e.g. those working outside of the creative sectors in areas like banking, catering, IT, law and others) can produce a space for networking, collaborating and skill sharing across digital and non-digital platforms. The authors conclude that there needs to be continued strategic leadership support for the Bangladeshi creative industry managers so that they are capable of delivering and communicating creative projects across diverse generations and audiences, which is often complicated by the lack of visibility to centralised access to technology and talent. This should also help to engage and include the Bangladeshi community within the growth of the UK creative economies in the future. Continuing with the theme of South Asian arts and culture in the UK, Jasjit Singh's paper 'What value South Asian arts in Britain' reports that even though South Asian arts forms play an important role in enabling audiences to participate in relevant arts, South Asian arts organisations continue to be required to articulate their value primarily as part of a commitment to 'diversity'. This paper presents some research evidence examining the cultural value of South Asian arts using four measures of their impact on: the economy; health and wellbeing; society; and education. The findings state that these arts can play an important role in engaging those who might be less likely to participate in arts activities. Also showing that some South Asian artists may not wish to be pigeonholed as purely 'South Asian' and others may wish to engage with South Asian arts because it provides them with a link to their heritage.

The next two articles have a Bollywood cinema industry connection. Giovanna Rampazzo's paper 'The Production of Ek Tha Tiger: a Marriage of Convenience between Bollywood and the Irish Film and Tourist Industries', examines a collaboration between the Irish and Bollywood film industries for the production of *Ek Tha Tiger* (2012) in Dublin. This case study draws on participant observation in the film's production, alongside interviews conducted with the film's producers and representatives of the Irish Film and Tourist Boards. Having *Ek Tha Tiger* set in Ireland represented a big leap forward in the country's attempts to secure Hindi film industry investments, providing a unique opportunity to showcase the beauty of Ireland to a vast number of potential Indian tourists. Hence, the film laid the foundation for future collaboration between Indian entertainment industries and Irish creative and cultural industries. The second Bollywood industry paper 'New Bollywood and the Emergence of a Production House culture' by Amrita Goswami, attempts to show how the Hindi film industry has paved the way for a corporate-led approach towards film production, distribution and circulation (New Bollywood). Goswami shows that in New Bollywood, production houses controlling the business of film production, distribution and circulation, are not exclusively in the business of making films alone; the film business is just one component of a larger audiovisual industry comprising of media and communications empires. She illustrates that the phenomenon of global media conglomeration which happened in the 1990s in Hollywood, took shape in the 2000s in India, thus opening up opportunities for screen convergence, where a film's earnings are not dependent on just its theatrical exhibition, but also through its release across platforms and screens (satellite TV, mobile, home video, etc.). This provides us with a useful insight into the contemporary workings of a major South Asian creative industry in the production of popular culture.

The fifth article presented in this special issue is 'Optimising the Contribution of Design to Innovation Performance in Indian small to medium enterprises (SMEs) – What roles for Culture,

Tradition, Policy and Skills?', co-authored by Simon Bolton, Lawrence Green and Bhavin Kothari. This essay commences by examining the growing body of evidence and commentary relating to the contribution of the creative industries – especially the design sector – to the innovation performance of firms and national economies. It moves on to explore trajectories in policy that have been elaborated as a means of supporting and fostering design, and provides examples and analysis of design promotion initiatives from across the globe. In line with the theme of this special issue, the article attempts to demonstrate how and in what ways do the creative industries and creative practitioners contribute to innovation performance in Indian SMEs. More specifically drawing out implications relating to issues of cultural diversity, demographics and regional identity for design-enabled innovation in Indian SMEs. India is experiencing rapid growth, and design is just one factor that will facilitate its acceleration. However, it is a factor that faces a unique set of challenges, which include: the orientation to design that is prevalent in India (importation and adaptation) must gradually shift in favour of indigenous design; and there is much space to blend traditional craft with contemporary design sensitivities, especially since India is uniquely well-placed possessing a rich heritage and culture.

The final research article is entitled 'Envisioning the Future: Financialization and the Indian Entertainment Industry Reports' by Nitin Govil. This work uses quite an imaginative presentation style drawing on and critiquing industry reports with a number of different graph illustrations. Govil argues that India's investment in the creative sector has been mobilized by future-oriented aesthetic strategies, which he details in his argument. His archive is the annual Indian entertainment industry brochure, now the standard gauge for business interest in the creative sector, produced by Indian business lobbies in collaboration with media industry confabs and international management consultancies. Govil considers that the rapidity of aesthetic transformation in the Indian entertainment industry reports, from simple to increasingly aggregated regimes of accuracy, is symptomatic of the compressed time-space of Asian modernity. He also posits that these reports conscript data to a new regime, designed not only to present a vision of the future, but motivated by the necessity of envisioning for tomorrow.

This special issue also contains some very interesting insights on the theme of creative and cultural industries from three 'Working Notes'. The first contribution is an interview-based working note from Emma Varughese entitled 'Bahrisons New Delhi: commerce and creativity in Khan Market'. This contribution gives us valuable insights into a book store in New Delhi's Khan Market, which has come to be known as Bahrisons. This book store's continuing success relies on the creative industries of domestic India, a sector that has undergone immense change post millennium. The interview conducted with the book store's CEO, explores issues of commerce in Khan Market and gives some fascinating facts into the manner in which books are selected, sold and marketed, which all takes place against the backdrop of New India.

The second Working Note is a short essay on 'Impacts of Funding in Digitising the Bangladesh Film Industry: Challenges Ahead', prepared by Muhammad Shajjad Ahsan. This essay shows that although the impacts of government funding in digitising the Bangladesh film industry is noticeable, the aspiration of growth to be expected has not yet been fully met. In-depth interviews with film industry professionals and secondary data insights are utilised to better understand productivity growth and business to business relations in the context of the Bangladesh Film Industry's digitisation project, revealing that this project was not completed within its original timeframe. However, this essay confirms that the Bangladesh Film Development Corporation's traditional production capability has now been integrated into its digital upgrade, which has been the main goal for this industry since 2003.

The third Working Note is by Catherine Casson entitled 'Creative Enterprise from the Medieval to the Modern Period: Alternative Perspectives'. This contribution presents an insightful review of two books that are linked to the special issue theme. The books by Denise Tsang (2015), *Entrepreneurial Creativity in a Virtual World* and by Karel Davids and Bert de Munck, eds. (2014), *Innovation and Creativity in Late Medieval and Early Modern European Cities* are compared and contrasted here. One interesting issue arising is that both books suggest that new and creative ideas can emerge out of both opportunity and necessity. For example, from the book *Innovation and Creativity in Late Medieval and Early Modern European Cities*, Casson highlights the fact that 'necessity' drove product innovation in woollen production in Florence in the fifteenth and sixteenth centuries. From the book *Entrepreneurial Creativity in a Virtual World*, Casson highlights the fact that the use of 'social media' for marketing purposes is now seen as a cost-effective way for small companies to promote goods or services. Casson's paper also demonstrates how both of these books make a strong contribution to the field of innovation and creativity. While not explicitly covering the geographical region of South Asia, both books address themes that appear in current research on innovation in a South Asian context.

The range and variety of articles and shorter pieces compiled in this special issue exemplify some important developments in the area of creativity and cultural industries research, especially in the context of South Asia. The essays have advanced our understanding of how these developments play out at various levels of analysis within different types of firms and other organisations, as well as providing some interesting policy perspectives to learn from in the future. We hope that researchers active in the fields of arts and humanities, business studies and social science disciplines may embrace some of the themes presented in the special issue and learn some new insights from the methodological approaches reported in a number of the articles. It is also hoped that this special issue stimulates more interesting future research into analysing creative and cultural industries, especially from a South Asian perspective.

Acknowledgements

We are extremely grateful to all our anonymous reviewers for providing invaluable comments and contributing their time to this special issue.

References

Aggestam, Maria. "Art-entrepreneurship in the Scandinavian Music Industry." *Entrepreneurship in the Creative Industries: An International Perspective*. Ed. C. Henry. Cheltenham: Edward Elgar, 2007. 30–53.

Cox, George. *Cox Review of Creativity in Business: Building on the UK's Strengths*. HM Treasury, 2005. <http://grips-public.mediactive.fr/knowledge_base/view/349/cox-review-of-creativity-in-business-building-on-the-uk-s-strengths/>.

Florida, Richard. *The Rise of the Creative Class: And How It's Transforming Work, Leisure, Community, and Everyday Life*. New York: Basic Books, 2002.

Swedberg Richard. "The Cultural Entrepreneur and the Creative Industries: Beginning in Vienna." *Journal of Cultural Economics* 30.4 (2006): 243–61.

UNCTAD. *Creative Economy Report: 2013 Special Edition*. UNDP, 2013. <http://www.unesco.org/culture/pdf/creative-economy-report-2013.pdf>.

Beyond the creative class, mapping the collaborative economy of Bangladeshi creative industries: Case study of *Oitij-jo*

Lipi Begum and Maher Anjum

ABSTRACT

This paper documents how the British Bangladeshi diaspora in the UK has been collaborating to contribute to the growth of the creative sector in the UK and in Bangladesh. Through case studies from the creative-start-up of Oitij-jo (February 2013) and subsequently the planning of its second project 'AKHON: Where is Bengal Now', this paper charts the collaborations between the culture and creative industries of Bengali heritage (film, photography, theatre, dance, music, art, architecture, textiles and fashion) involved in the project between 2013 and 2016. The authors question widely used policy notions of 'the creative class' and 'creative clustering' and explore the collaborative economy model for the growth of Bangladeshi cultural and creative industries. Using infographics and netnographic interviews, the paper maps out advantages and disadvantages of collaboration linked to digital and non-digital peer-to-peer skills sharing and entrepreneurship. It concludes with the next steps for Oitij-jo and discusses the managerial implications for sustainability of its future projects.

Bangladeshis in creative Britain

The UK's creative sector is one of the most consistently successful sectors in the country. It is estimated[1] that between 2008 and 2012 the UK creative sector contributed £71 billion to the economy, representing an increase of 15.6% compared to the overall economy which grew by 5.6% (DCMS 7). Given the sector's growth and future growth potential in fashion, digital industries, software development, architecture and performance arts, this paper explores how the British Bangladeshi diaspora in the UK have been collaborating with their counterparts in Bangladesh and globally to innovate, be motivated and contribute to the growth of the creative sector in the UK and in Bangladesh.

British Bangladeshi's have been travelling and settling in Britain since the eighteenth and nineteenth century as *lascars* (sailors) and *ayahs* (nurses, maids) (Visram 9). Post World War II, men arrived along with their compatriots from other commonwealth countries to cities across the UK to run services and rebuild them (Visram 9). It was not until the birth of Bangladesh and the change in UK immigration rules of the 'right of entry' in 1971, that Bangladeshi men increasingly settled in the UK and started to bring their families over (Somerville et al. 2009). In particular, the 1980s saw a surge of the Bangladeshi community settling from Bangladesh to the UK (Li 25) and since then Bangladeshi's have been integrating into the UK community through education and work.

In accordance to the 2011[2] Census, 0.8% of UK's population or 447,000 people in the UK are of British Bangladeshi origin. Degree level qualification among the 16–24 year old age group is proportionally higher than any of the other age groups (Lymperopoulou 2014). It is estimated the percentage of 'no qualification' saw a significant drop between 2001 and 2011 from 47% to 28%, a difference of 19% within a decade. In 2011 the overall attainment difference between the genders also decreased (men 24% and women 33%) and among the 16–24 year old age group there is virtually no difference (Lymperopoulou 2015). In fact, in 2014 the number of British Bangladeshi youngsters achieving five good GCSEs was higher (61%) than Pakistani (51%) or indigenous White British populations (54%) (Li 25).

In spite of the advances made in education for the British Bangladeshi population of UK, majority of them still live in low-income social housing concentrated in London (Alzubaidi et al. 2013). Although the distribution of income has risen for those of Bangladeshi households than previously (Li 25) the levels of economic activity amongst the British Bangladeshi community remain slow. According to the 2011 Census, men of Bangladeshi origin were 53% likely to be working in low-skilled jobs and 67% for women. Fifty-four of men in employment worked in part-time jobs and less than thirty hours per week and 12% worked in jobs that were less than 15 h a week. For women the figures are just as striking, 56 and 23%, respectively (ONS 13).

Overall, British Bangladeshi's have come a long way since the 1980s. The anecdotal evidence is that South Asian communities have a preference for professions in law, medicine, accountancy or education. The creative sectors are not seen as a real form of employment or source of income (Evans 102). Yet, a new generation of settled British Bangladeshis are breaking into non-traditional creative sectors and are increasingly becoming renowned for their creativity. For example winner of The BBC Great British Bake Off (2015), Nadiya Hussain and Akram Khan MBE the dancer are two particular instances here. The participation of Bangladeshis within the creative economy of the UK is under-recognised. Creative practices of theatre, dance, drama, poetry, textile and crafts that have a long tradition in Bangladesh and Bengal are not known, understood, or are reflective of the lives of the community in the UK. Additionally, Bangladesh is the second largest garments and apparel exporter globally (Saxena 4), however this achievement of the garments sector is tainted by recent tragic factory incidences of Tazreen and Rana Plaza. It can be said that the creative sector is one of the fastest growing sectors in the UK, yet has had very little impact on the British Bangladeshi diaspora community.

It is within this backdrop and vacuum of creative Bangladeshi/Bengali[3] imagery that we set the discussion for the rest of the paper. In this paper, through the case study of Oitij-jo, a not-for-profit platform, we showcase creativity motivated by the creative heritage of Bangladeshi and Bengali origin. Oitij-jo illustrates how contrary to the negativity of a low-skilled, low innovation image, Bangladeshi and Bengali heritage is historically and currently rich in creativity and high in skills. We discuss how a lack of cultural understanding of what often constitutes a worthwhile creative investment in the Bangladeshi community by policy-makers and funders, hinders the growth of Bangladeshi creative industries. We explore the cultural relevance of policy notions, such as creative class (Florida 2002) and creative clustering (De Propis and Hyponnen 2008) and the benefits of going beyond these approaches towards collaborative economy models (Stokes et al. 2014), which support greater skills management and growth of the British Bangladeshi creative industries and its practitioners.

Methodology

Oitij-jo (www.oitijjo.org) was founded in October 2012 by architect Ruhul Abdin (male, age 25–40) independent consultant Maher Anjum (female, age 41–60). Independent British Bangladeshi photographer Enamul Hoque (male, age 41-60) and Abbas Nokahsteh (male, age 41-60) founder of Openvizor (www.openvizor.com an international non-profit arts and cultural organisation currently working in over fifteen countries). Oitij-jo in Bangla means heritage, however the naming reflects a dynamic rather than static and stagnant past. It can be summarised as a heritage that is learning from and looking at the past for the present, to better develop and deliver in the future. Oitij-jo started out with the vision to present creative excellence and achievement of Bengali traditions in the arts and crafts, to enrich and enhance the present perception of Bengali arts and crafts and to ensure prosperity of lively arts and crafts practices (Oitij-jo 2013, 2015).

Oitij-jo's initial steering committee in 2012 included Runi Khan (female, age 61–80) of CulturePot Global a performing arts company (https://www.facebook.com/CulturepotGlobal/) and John Baker (male, age 61–80) a voluntary sectors worker with over fifty years experience working for the borough of Tower Hamlets in East London. For Oitij-jo 2013, support was also received from the then High Commissioner of Bangladesh to the UK, Quayes Mohamed Mijarul. The Oitij-jo collective went on to register as a not-for profit company in October 2013 with Ruhul, Maher, Abbas and Enamul registered as founding directors and also John Baker later in 2015.

In this chapter through the start-up journey of Oitij-jo UK, we illustrate a series of anecdotal case studies and infographics to demonstrate how open platforms like Oitij-jo can enhance a wealth of networks necessary for nurturing entrepreneurship and growth. This is irrespective of whether creatives fit into the classification of popular policy approaches such as 'the creative class' (Florida 2002). The case illustrates the challenges and barriers of creative collaboration, concluding with ways forward for the growth and planning of Oitij-jo's second project *AKHON/Where is Bengal NOW*.

The information was gathered from the inaugural Oitij-jo event that took place in February 2013 and the feedback that followed in 2011 and in 2015. It also includes the feedback from the most recent event in March 2016 to launch the planned 2017/2018 festival. We applied a netnographic (Kozinets 2015) approach to data collection. We conducted qualitative online interviews with artists and planners behind the Oitij-jo event and culturally contextualised online information on Oitij-jo from its Facebook page, Twitter account, official website and gathered online interviews. We also documented projects related to Bangladeshi heritage that have taken place as a result of volunteer networking and conversations at the Oitij-jo events. In keeping with the netnographic philosophy, the information is visually contextualised using infographics to illustrate the possibilities of creative collaboration and to make data accessible to a wider audience.

A cultural perspective on creative class and creative clustering

Firstly, it is important for us to understand what the role and impact of creative industries is to the UK's economy and as a nation. It is estimated that the number of jobs in the creative industries (including both creative and support jobs) increased by 5.5% between 2013 and 2014 to 1.8 million jobs. Total employment in the creative economy across the UK increased by 5.0% between 2013 and 2014 (2.6–2.8 million jobs), compared with a 2.1% increase in the total number of jobs in the wider UK economy over the same period (DCMS 5).

Over the last decade, this growth has been reflected in policy dialogues and debates taking place in the UK and increasingly across the globe. This global shift is charted in the move away from the term cultural industries to creative industries (Evans 2009). Culture and cultural industries are no longer instruments of the nation-state, confined to broadcasting, arts and heritage but global creative industries. In 2004 UNCTAD (United Nations Conference on Trade and Development) said that creative industries were the crossroads between the arts, business and technology (UNCTAD 4). This re-definition is also a reflection of the discussion by proponents of the 'creative city' e.g. work of Florida (2002) and other creative city advocates (Landry 2000; Nichols-Clarke 2004). These advocates believed that a 'tolerant', 'open' and vibrant place attracts creative and knowledge workers (Evans 1009) and what Florida terms the 'creative class'. In essence it is this notion of the creative class that started the discussion on creative industries and creative sectors.

If we take a step back, Florida (2002) argues that highly educated creative professionals such as architects, artists and non-fiction writers are catalysts to city development. Florida argues that the three drivers of creative class are technology, talent and tolerance (3Ts) and that cities which achieve these 3Ts attract high-tech investment and growth. However, Florida's approach did not take into account regional development, or the diversity of the communities who share and compete for creative spaces within the city. A community within a city may receive investment on the basis of Florida's 3Ts, however this overlooks other creative communities in the same city who lack visibility within mainstream creative education, socio-economic mobility and ultimately equal access to technology, talent and tolerance.

This dominant notion of the 'creative class' as an answer to the sustainable competitiveness of a city has been challenged by those who have looked at unevenly distributed cultural industries, the wide range of industries that constitute cultural industries and the differences within them (e.g. fashion, film, music, TV, games, advertising). However many policy dialogues still follow the hegemonised debate of the creative class. Pratt (1) calls this the normative policy debate or the 'Xerox' policy. It is salient in Florida's work that policy needs to take into account the uniqueness of a context, however Pratt (2) argues popularisation of the work of Florida's 3T is an example of how diversity is still to be understood. These normative policy dialogues are typically seen in most widely used policy initiatives, such as the creative cluster model (De Propis and Hyponnen 2008).

According to De Propris and Hyponnen (258) a creative cluster is a place that brings together a community of 'creative people' who share an interest in novelty but not necessarily in the same subject: a catalysing place where people, relationships, ideas and talents can spark each other; an environment that offers diversity, stimuli and freedom of expression; a thick, open and ever-changing network of inter-personal exchanges that nurture individual's uniqueness and identity. The advantages of creative clustering include creative spillovers that lead to future collaborations and innovations, regional and transnational economic development, increase in demand and co-location opportunities via networks close to each other, or social media.

Creative clustering poses as a solution to its lesser creative and scientific roots of strategic clustering (Porter 1990),[4] however it still operates within a scientific framework that favours a science policy to culture and creative industries (Pratt 2009). The use of creative clustering is widely used in cultural policy-making and has now been adopted by economically driven industries such as real estate, science, sport and I.T (Mommaas 2009; Pratt 2009). Mommaas (2009) argues that the term has given rise to an appealing agenda but at the same time hides 'a confusing and tense complexity' (Mommaas 47). Mommaas argues that creative clustering notions are not made explicit and the histories of creative clustering strategies are diverse and complex.

It is not to say that we cannot learn from the notion of the creative class (2002) and creative clustering (De Propis and Hyponnen 2008). For instance digital co-location advantages of creative clustering can be combined with geographic spillover and silo-breaking advantages of Porter's strategy-orientated clustering approach. For cultural creative industries that are emergent, diverse and starting from an unequal footing (in terms of investment and access to growth) policy notions such as the collaborative economy (Stokes et al. 5) are better suited.

Collaborative economy definitions are varied and are constantly evolving, however the main idea around the collaborative economy, or the peer-to-peer/sharing economy is the idea of access (Stokes et al. 5) compared to the ownership approach of the three 3Ts. 'Collaborative economies encourage decentralised networks over centralised institutions, and unlock wealth (with and without money). They make use of idle assets and create new marketplaces. In doing so, many also challenge traditional ways of doing business, rules and regulations' (Stokes et al. 7). Examples of this approach are brands like Air BnB, Ebay and Massive Online Courses. The ideas which make up a collaborative economy are not new and overlap and extend policy notions such as creative class, creative clustering and south Asian cultural approaches to frugal innovation like *Jugaad* (Radjou et al. 2012). However, the emphasis placed upon a decentralised and open approach makes it an attractive policy approach for those looking to overcome socio-political and economic barriers to public funding, and those seeking to build informal networks via better and quicker access to technology and skills and ideas exchange at little cost.

The following section through the illustrative infographics and online interviews demonstrates how collaborative economy models are useful for overcoming social and economic barriers to reaching out to creatives within disparate markets. The case contextualises the limitation of popular creative industry policy approaches, such as creative clustering and creative class approach for the British Bangladeshi creative and cultural industries.

Visualising Oitij-jo 'Past Present Future'

'Past, Present, Future' was the title for the first event in 2013. The event engaged with over seventy artists of the Bengali diaspora and was received well (see www.oitijjo.org). The first

Infographic 1. The story of Oitij-jo 2013, created by Noemi Zajzon©.

event took place at the Bargehouse, South Bank, London in February 2013. The following infographic visualises the Oitij-jo landscape.

As seen in Infographic 1, Oitij-jo mapped out the key cultural industries of Bangladesh and incorporated them into the planning processes of Oitij-jo's inaugural event 'Past-Present-Future' in 2013. This event was held over three days and was attended by over 1500 people. The infographic above illustrates how the event, financed mostly by independent charities and British Bangladeshi entrepreneurs, brought together key cultural industries of Bangladeshi heritage including: literature, visual arts, photography, fashion & textiles, film and art. These practices were supported through the open platforms of interactive displays, performances, talks, debates and exhibitions.

The first event relied on volunteers participating on a pro-bono basis. Volunteers came from all backgrounds, ages and experiences to put the event together. The manner in which the event was planned worked well for some volunteers, however it was conflicting with others. We found that, success factors were also barriers and were predominantly related to the challenges surrounding informal and decentralised peer-to-peer skills sharing, entrepreneurship and leadership approaches. The following section maps out and further explains this dialectical process of learning.

Peer-to-peer skills sharing and entrepreneurship

Oitij-jo's first event was an open and collaborative platform. Infographic 2 essentially illustrates the key role volunteers played in this process. This decentralised and open approach was undertaken to cut the costs of organising an event with access to limited funding, a short space of time in Central London and within a large venue. As illustrated in Infographic 2, volunteers can be categorised as follows: volunteers from a practicing creative background; volunteers from a non-creative background but interested in the creative sector; professionals who were keen to build new networks; students both creative and non-creative. Infographic 2

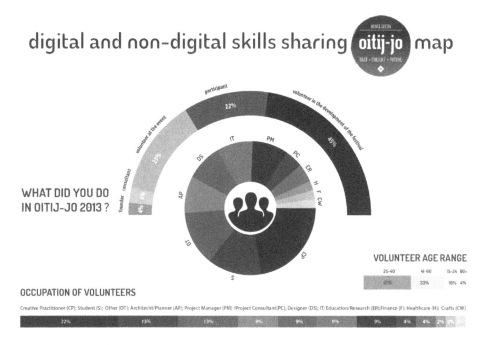

Infographic 2. Digital and non-digital skills sharing map, created by Noemi Zajzon©.

depicts how voluntary collaborations between over seventy artists and non-artists, across platforms took place during the planning of the event, and in as little as six months.

To be specific, creatives in this context included those who were directly working as creative practitioners such as musicians, dancers, film-makers, photographers, writers and curators. Non-creatives in this context included those working outside of the creative sectors, example those working in banking, law, healthcare, catering, logistics, I.T, Management among others. What Infographic 2 illustrates is how Oitij-jo created a space for networking, collaborating and skills sharing across digital (social media and email) and non-digital (face-to-face during events and planning meetings) platforms between those already engaged and new to the creative sector (in this context creatives and non-creatives). The volunteers, creatives and non-creatives also came through to Oitij-jo through their collaboration with other networks like BritBangla, Brick Lane Circle, Swadhinata Trust, British Bangladeshi Fashion Council, Emerald Network and a long list of individuals.

One of the benefits from the volunteering process for many was being able to informally exchange and learn creative skills. During an online interview a non-Bangladeshi art student from Malta, expressed the opinion that getting involved in Oitij-jo was 'a way to get involved in the local art scene whilst undertaking his masters in Culture Criticism and Curation in London' (male, age 41–60). Another non-Bangladeshi textile artist who regularly works on arts projects within her Bangladeshi neighbourhood in East-London, said during an interview 'I found it an accessible platform to connect with others doing similar projects' (female, age 41–60). Here the non-Bangladeshi artist and the art student are examples of how creative practitioners gained greater awareness and understanding of creative practices related to Bangladeshi heritage through volunteering at Oitij-jo.

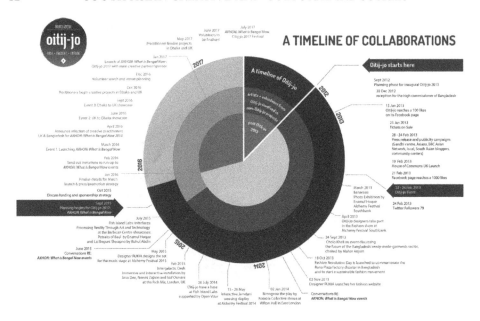

Infographic 3. A timeline of collaborations, created by Noemi Zajzon©.

Other advantages of peer-to-peer skills sharing included new and established artists gaining confidence from the professional and social relationships formed over what was an intense period of planning. One emerging fashion designer (female, age 25–40,) explained during an online interview how 'being involved with the members of Oitij-jo really helped to be more confident in talking to potential clients and like-minded people and expressing myself and my work'. For other artists, it provided them with the confidence to nurture existing ideas and 'learn more about events management (female, age 25–40, online interview)' and the 'business and planning side of things' (male, 25–40, online interview), and importantly skills sharing between creative practitioners and volunteers beyond the Oitij-jo event. This is seen within the timeline illustrated in Infographic 3.

Infographic 3 maps the parallel and ongoing creative dialogues sparked between artists and volunteers throughout the event planning process and after the event. These dialogues took place between the period 2012 and 2015 and are ongoing as part of the planning process for the next Oitij-jo festival in 2017/2018.

Infographic 3 illustrates the rich, intertwining and complex post-Oitij-jo 2013 collaborations. These collaborations took place as a result of creative practitioners and volunteers directly and indirectly working with and engaging with those they met through Oitij-jo 2013. For some it wasn't easy to separate how they were motivated or which connections they made before or after the Oitij-jo event, however their participation in Oitij-jo became a motivator to remain engaged with the Bangladeshi cultural and creative industries. One of the co-founders (male 25–40) explained over Gmail chat how

> It was interesting to see other collaborations emerge from the festival especially connections between Enamul Hoque [male, age 41–60, photographer] and Leesa Gazi [female, 41–60 theatre and TV producer] and some of the young volunteers now working very closely with artists, one volunteer [female, age 16–24, Business Management undergraduate student] is working

for the big dancer Akram Khan. The projects we have been developing in collaboration (such as the street kid's film) with Openvizor and The Rainbow Collective has been fascinating. Another development I feel was a great output, was the ability to network with other artists and support each other.

Skills sharing and entrepreneurial endeavours were not always driven by the need for artistic expression alone and were also borne out of a sense of individual desire to enter into competitive creative industries and make projects work within time and resource constraints and limited management direction. One volunteer in an interview stated 'I felt left out, there was no time to attend to me, but I believed in the cause so kept going' (female, age 25–40). Another British-Bangladeshi community artist describes how 'Bangladeshi's are naturally entrepreneurial but time constraints are de-motivating for those looking to experience what it is like to work in a creative career' (male, age 25–40). These entrepreneurial endeavours were also catalysed by the hallmark of collaborative economy activities i.e. the Internet and social media (Botsman and Rogers 2010), which enabled an intricate network of connections to occur within a short period of time – this is illustrated in Infographic 4.

The established nature of the London arts and creative industries scene meant the geographic location of London was an attractive advantage for creatives to connect. However it was the co-location advantages of social media and word-of-mouth simultaneously, which played a bigger role in the crowdsourcing of volunteers who did not always frequent the established arts London scene and were looking for accessible work experience

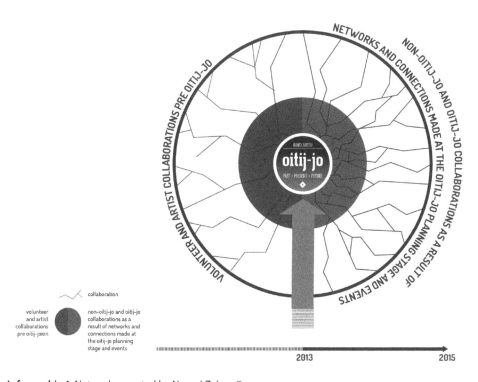

Infographic 4. Networks, created by Noemi Zajzon©.

in the creative industries. The use of technology to source creatives and volunteers for the event proved successful. Through emails, social media (LinkedIn, Facebook and Twitter) and personal websites. The volunteers in the organising team were able to draw together three artists in film, five in fashion, fourteen in theatre and music, two in dance, four in photography, six in creative education, two in art, five in literature, four in sustainable fashion and textile including twenty volunteers interested in the arts who assisted in the development of the event.

The Oitij-jo Facebook page was an accessible and low-cost marketing tool. It was able to reach the volunteers and over a thousand followers within four months. (https://www.facebook.com/oitijjolondon/). Facebook helped communicate a message of openness, inclusivity and open-access and common sharing of images and text (Botsman and Rogers 2010; Stokes et al. 2014) between volunteers and artists – all of which are necessary for collaborative economy activities to flourish. For some artists the publicity received from the Oitij-jo event was more important than the consumption of their work through ticket sales. Those who could not come to the events, engaged with the cultural and creative industries of Bangladesh through accessible interactions through Facebook likes, follows, LinkedIn connections and Tweets. According to one of the social media managers for events (male, age 25–40), 'Facebook was a great public relations tool to spread the Oitij-jo message quickly and reach out to wider and younger Bangladeshi and non-Bangladeshi audience'. Social media allowed artists to consume other artist's work and come together to engage with new cultural ideas.

The interaction over social media blurred those who were consuming arts and those producing the art. Ownership became access. This is seen where those with limited experience of the creative industries were introduced to Bangladeshi cultural and creative industries through Oitij-jo. One non-Bangladeshi cultural ambassador (male, age 60+) in the community states:

> I have developed an appreciation of the work of the Rainbow Collective and Komola Collective, and now consider myself a working friend of both…Through all these contacts and friends I've been 'introduced' to the world of Bengali music, especially to the work of Khiyo and Lokhi Terra. Numerous websites and Facebook pages account the activities of the groups I've mentioned, and a couple of short texts credited to me have appeared in 'The Geographical Magazine', photography by Enamul.

Aside from generating awareness and inviting the community to engage, technology was also a logistical tool for setting up ticket selling platforms and managing sales. The usage of an Eventbrite platform facilitated the sale of tickets for the three-day event and allowed participants and guests from across the globe to learn about the programme and access their tickets. According to one of the organisers (male, age 25–40) during an interview:

> Facebook was definitely a big tool used to promote and engage with the festival attendants, and twitter was also relatively useful. Communication streams internally and externally were managed through the Internet, as well as using the website to promote events at the festival. It was where people could purchase tickets. The relative ease of the tools such as Facebook and website with a content management system, meant we could keep costs down and do a lot of the marketing and promoting ourselves.

Next steps: Beyond borders

Based on the lessons learnt from volunteers and organisers from the first event, planning is seen as a priority. The next series of events will be hosted across an eighteen-month period as a build-up to the final event to allow planning to happen in incremental steps (can be seen in Infographic 3). This period would also be utilised for raising funds and creating events to build and attract a wider audience and reach for the next festival planned for 2017/2018. Volunteer feedback from the first event included the need to create internship opportunities for volunteers in the creative sectors, as well as, project dissemination strategies that incorporate schools, colleges and community centres in local and regional areas. It was also observed that engagement is necessary from the wider artistic community and a greater number of artists. Therefore a key consideration in moving forward is to develop artist residencies to build material for the next festival, which would also require further financial backing.

In order to reach out to the wider creative community, the steering committee decided to focus on expanding the term Bangladeshi to Bengali heritage. The first event captured both Bengali and Bangladeshi heritage, however many felt this didn't come across and the term Bengali was more inclusive and sustainable for the long-term future of Oitij-jo. As a result of this change, and various planning meetings and conversations, the second London Oitij-jo festival theme was agreed as 'AKHON: Where is Bengal Now?'

AKHON: Where is Bengal Now centres on the importance of the creative industry as a critical tool for transformation towards a cohesive and engaged society. The theme for the festival is rooted in visual and craft cultures in present-day Bengal, which consists of Bangladesh and West Bengal, India. Maintaining the original Oitij-jo philosophy, the event will present a diverse range of disciplines including literature, visual arts, photography, film, music, performance, theatre & dance, spoken word, architecture, design, fashion & textiles and critical discourse. The inclusion of Bengal opens up the platform to those who identify with the rich Bengali cultural heritage before the India partition (1947). It taps into the creative industries of a regional Bengali heritage, a distinctive identity often overshadowed by a national Indian identity. This would also metaphorically open up artistic borders, break down cultural and artistic silos between West Bengal in India and Bangladesh and increase the reach for social capital amongst the Bengali creative community – all of which are key drivers of the collaborative economy approach (Stokes et al. 2014).

The launch event for 'AKHON: Where is Bengal Now' took place at the Rich Mix Centre (www.richmix.org), a community space in East London on the 24 March 2016. The event was centred on performances from four female musicians of Bengali heritage (Gouri Chowdhury 25–40; Sohni Alam 25–40; Sarah Sayeed 25–40; DJ DEBONAIR 21–25). The event introduced Oitij-jo to old and new audiences and the host for the night (female, age 25–40, TV host) introduced the aim and objectives for Oitij-jo 2017/2018. The event attracted over 80 people and the inclusion of Bengal heritage was seen as a positive step forward. A West Bengali audience member (male, age 25–40) felt the mixture of audience ranging from young to old, Bangladeshi and Bengali, singers, local community members and those from outside of East London was a positive sight. However the challenge around receiving mainstream press coverage and widening audience reach and interest for financial investment still remain a barrier.

A diverse audience at 'Akhon: What is Bengal Now' reinforced some of the best practice ways of working from Oitij-jo's inaugural event in 2013. The diverse audience at the March 2016 launch event relied heavily on decentralised and informal digital word of mouth communication across Oitij-jo's personal social media platforms and Rich Mix's website and email database. These non-physical networks (volunteer social media accounts) generated by the event challenged the popular policy idea that centralised and physical networks are the only drivers to building a creative community (such as creative class, clustering and creative cities). One of the key drivers of access to the 2013 event for artists and audience was the informal networks created through the Internet. Therefore it was recognised that one of the ways to build on the success of Oitij-jo 2013 for Oitij-jo 2017/2018 is to capitalise on the decentralised network capabilities of the collaborative economy approach, for example utilising the capabilities of extending reach quickly through volunteer social media networks. However it was noted that future success is also dependent on a blended approach of utilising both technological and non-technological networks.

Although, technology allowed the project to grow at a rapid rate through various platforms at a low cost, some of the challenges of raising awareness around the event were not alleviated by accessible marketing tools like social media. The heavy dependence on social media meant networks were constrained to younger audiences, personal networks of those already engaged in the project and users of Facebook and Twitter. Skills sharing gained the most strength during the physical planning stage. However it was difficult to measure skills sharing via social media posts and it was difficult to engage the audience through tools such as Twitter, which only gained seventy followers. Furthermore, even though the strategic location choice of an East London community space for the 'Akhon: Where is Bengal Now' launch was based on the feedback to make the event physically accessible to the community, it proved challenging to get the desired audience numbers. Without links to formal centralised networks such as public funding, local council and government support, the advantages of the blended approach of securing a good geographic location (with good community reach) alongside digital co-location was difficult to realise. The launch event received little mainstream press and investment leads. The heavy reliance on unpaid skills meant it was difficult to maintain a post-event social media strategy required to build on and evaluate the impact of the event. It became difficult to gather the data required to put together mainstream funding applications that sought accountability. According to one of the organisers (male, 25–40 age) interviewed,

> it is cost effective, it makes it easier to implement, but it also means because there is so much content out there now that tactics used need to be fresh and engaging, so the challenge will be to come up with strategies that inspire new audiences and promote the festival participants in the best possible light.

To undertake these strategies further, ongoing volunteer support is required, and for this support to be sustainable in the long-term, funding is required. One volunteer working on the fashion design and textiles strand of Oitij-jo 2017/2018 explained over email, how she would like to take part in Oitij-jo events and sees it as an essential platform to promote the practice of artists, and for encouraging the Bangladeshi community in London to engage with the creative sectors. However she believes, given that artists are already struggling to receive paid work in London, 'without a small budget for materials it would prove difficult to take part' (Female, age 25–40, textile artist). Furthermore, feedback from several unsuccessful public funding applications for *Akhon: Where is Bengal Now* reinforced the lack of understanding of diversity and complexity of collaborative economy approaches by public funders. One funding body was unwilling to fund 'staff/volunteer costs' and to support several 'wider projects' (anonymous public funder, 2016) and another required centralised outputs linked to narrow outcomes which purported to alleviate 'poverty' in troubled economically deprived regions of the UK, or addressed the complex issues of 'religious radicalisation' (anonymous public funder, 2016). It became clear that creative industries, which are seen to reside outside of politically topical and popular policy arenas, are unlikely to receive support, financial or otherwise.

For Oitij-jo the success of future event relies on how volunteer skills and entrepreneurial exchanges are rewarded through continuous support and engagement, both digital and non-digital across generations with diverse political and social views. For this to be successful, large-scale funding is required. With arts funding being cut across the UK and particularly London (Harvey 7), public funding remains a barrier to success. For instance, to register as a charity with the Charity Commission, it is now necessary to show at least £5000 in the bank of the organisation. Therefore fundraising needs to be sought and based on a portfolio approach.

One of the advantages of a collaborative economy approach is that it lends well to moving away from centralised fundraising approaches. Thus, a collaborative funding approach is perceived to be a possible way forward where funding can be crowd-sourced online and offline with a portfolio of key sponsors. Successful examples of this are crowd-sourced projects as seen through the emergence of crowd-funding marketplaces like CrowdCube and Indigogo. Other non-western examples include Projeckt.co a crowd-funding start-up in Bangladesh. Projeckt.co builds on the culture of giving in Bangladesh to empower creative community artists and entrepreneurs in Bangladesh who struggle to raise finance through public routes (see http://projekt.co). With a crowd-funding approach there is also the opportunity for sponsors to co-create with the artists for unique collaborations and innovations to take place.

Crowdfunding is a feasible option for Oitij-jo to promote and streamline geographic collaboration with technology. Through a crowd-sourced platform, the Oitij-jo team plan to engage with physical art practices and digital methods of preparation for the 2017/2018 festival to gain a wider physical and digital reach. Plans include an open call or commissioning process on the crowd-funding platform to develop work directly with artists/designers/performers; select practitioners and invite them to exhibit and perform at the event; organising physical residency for creative practitioners from Bangladesh to UK and UK to Bangladesh and taking the events outside of London to other parts of the UK. The collaborative approach would also be augmented by linking with platforms like the 'SASIAN Journey' set up recently by Asian Heritage Foundation (www.asianheritagefoundation.org) in association with the Self Employed Women's Association. The SASIAN Journey platform brings together representatives to explore creativity and design led innovations that better link geo-political regions. For SASIAN Journey, connecting with South Asian diaspora is a core area of focus, therefore an opportunity for Oitij-jo to collaborate. Collaboration opportunities create a way forward, however the barriers to public funding still remain. Creating high quality content, planning, managing platforms and introducing volunteers to collaborative practices require initial financial investments and skills interventions, to train and support the project managers on financial and non-financial processes of the project.

In conclusion a collaborative economy approach of disparate activities can come together, irrespective of normative visibility of technology, talent and ownership within a community. However collaborative economy approaches still fall outside of normative policy-making debates and remain a challenge for policy-makers (Stokes et al. 2014), as the success of such projects are difficult to measure immediately. They do not lend well to immediate or 'Xerox' (Pratt 2009) policy transfer often required to attract public investment. What Oitij-jo's journey also reveals is that greater levels of documentation of Bangladeshi creative projects are required to help policy-makers understand the grassroots collaborative economy approaches taking place in the community. To avoid repeating a Xerox policy approach, not only is it essential to understand best practices but also an understanding of the diverse challenges, so that this knowledge can be transferred to education and funding policies which seek to connect and situate the UK Bangladeshi community within the opportunities of the growing UK creative economy.

It can be seen from the Oitij-jo project that the collaborative economy is an emergent process. For many of the artists and volunteers involved it was not a straightforward process, there were moments of satisfaction and frustration, moments of entrepreneurship driven by desperation and others moments driven by creativity. Volunteers made these reflections only after the event. Greater moments of satisfaction for volunteers came about after the event through individual and group collaborations between volunteers and artists. This can be seen within with projects like *Intergalactic Desh* (www.londonsartistquarter.org/content/jane-h-dee/intergalactic-desh), *Portraits of Baul* (www.interfaces.fishislandlabs.com) and *Birongona the Play* (www.komola.co.uk) (highlighted within Infographic 3). Collaborations that happened after the inaugural festival in 2013 demonstrate the emergent nature of successful volunteer engagement. As one delivery team member said over email 'getting involved is simple but requires a lengthy process of continual engagement' (male, artist, age 25–40).

For managers, a successful engagement process not only includes the planning, managing and engaging artists and volunteers, but also the consistent strive to involve and engage public and private funders looking to support such projects. Thereby continual strategic leadership support is required for Bangladeshi creative industry managers to deliver and communicate creative projects across diverse generations and audiences, which are often complicated by the lack of visibility to centralised access to technology, talent and tolerance. With time and budget constraints, managers cannot always focus beyond the task at hand, therefore investment needs to go into digital and non-digital cross-cultural leadership training support for managers. This is essential for supporting creative industry managers and creative leaders in the community who are constantly striving to engage and include the Bangladeshi community within the growth of the UK creative economies with limited resources and access to skills.

Oitij-jo was and is a platform for nurturing collaborative learning. Many of the non-Bangladeshi artists involved in the Oitij-jo project found it to be a platform to reflect on their own heritage, against others, and a way to learn and value similarities and differences. For these artists, prior informal networks built through community, education and art practices catalysed their cultural learning. However, this wasn't the case for emerging Bangladeshi creatives who had limited prior networks to the creative industries. Yet, it can be said, that access to networks through platforms like Oitij-jo and advances in education made within the Bangladeshi community indicate potential growth and opportunity for network building through cross-cultural and collaborative learning. This opportunity calls for managers to push for policy, which takes into account continual investment in the understanding of collaborative approaches and tools (such as digital and non-digital channels) that can create networks for better social integration. Furthermore, what Oitij-jo highlights is that a collaborative and decentralised approach to learning is essential for the development of both the British Bangladeshi creative community and the future of the development of UK creative industries. As this approach does not only rely on ownership approaches but access to creative and cultural environments, it allows better scope for the British Bangladeshi community to participate and add to the diversity and innovation of the growing UK creative economy.

Notes

1. Figures on the creative industries are based on what the DCMS 2016 report classifies as experimental estimates of the value of the Creative Economy. These figures are not absolute and are what the Code of Practice for Official Statistics defines as Experimental Official Statistics, undergoing evaluation and review each year. For further details on methodology, see the methodology section of the full report.
2. It was not possible to include up-to-date statistics on the Bangladeshi community with regards to education and the creative industries, as there was limited data available on the topic. Where possible, estimates are provided and statistics are treated as quality measures to be built upon by stakeholders, refer to previous note.
3. We use Bengali and Bangladeshi interchangeably in this paper. Bengali refers to the historical identity of Bangladesh when it belonged to the region of Bengal in India, and when the region shared its identity across west Bengal and East Bengal (which later became East Pakistan after partition during the Indian Independence movement) before Indian independence/partition in 1947. In this paper, we mostly choose to use the term Bangladeshi to reinforce and to de-stigmatise the Bangladeshi cultural identity, which has been overshadowed by Indo-Pak relations since Bangladesh's independence from Pakistan in 1971. Yet, we recognise and appreciate that Bangladesh's cultural identity is inextricably linked to Bengali heritage post-partition and shared across west Bengal in India and Bangladesh, therefore we use these terms interchangeably.
4. Clustering is a strategic management approach popularised by management scholar Michael Porter. Porter defined clusters as geographical concentrations of interconnected companies and institutions within a particular field, an array of linked industries and other entities important to competition (Porter 1990). Porter argues that if countries are to remain competitive; related industries need to stay geographically close together. The reasons being, nations are likely to increase competitiveness if specialised skills and industries are clustered together to drive greater levels of competition, innovation and growth between them.

Acknowledgements

The authors would like to thank all those involved in the development and continual support of Oitij-jo from its inception to where it is now. Particular thanks goes to Noemi Zajzon for compiling the infographics. Noemi first started with Oitij-jo in 2013 and her support for it continues. Noemi Zajzon is a researcher and designer living in London. Her practice is based around curatorial, exhibition production and graphic design work and driven by an interest in creative engagement and socio-anthropological implications of spatial design. She trained to design spaces that challenge the way stories are told in the public realm, including exhibitions, community-centred projects and city narratives. She contributed to the development of Oitij-jo 2013 and supported the team with visual aids, like the infographics in the publication.

Disclosure statement

No potential conflict of interest was reported by the authors.

References

Alzubaidi, Haider, Carr, Jane, Councell, Rachel, and Johnson, G. Households below Average Income an Analysis of the Income Distribution 1994/95 – 2011/12. Department of Trade and Pensions UK. Jun. 2013. Web. 1 Sep. 2015. <https://www.gov.uk/government/uploads/system/uploads/attachment_data/file/206778/full_hbai13.pdf>.

Botsman Rachel, and Roo Rogers. *What's Mine is Yours: How Collaborative Consumption is Changing the Way We Live*. New York, NY: Harper Collins, 2010.

DCMS. *UK Creative Industries Economic Estimates*. Jan. 2016. Web. 1 Sep. 2015. <http://www.thecreativeindustries.co.uk/media/252528/ukti_creative_industries_action_plan_aw_rev_3-0_spreads.pdf>.

DCMS. *UK Creative Industries International Strategies*. Jan. 2014. Web. 1 Sep. 2015. <http://www.thecreativeindustries.co.uk/media/252528/ukti_creative_industries_action_plan_aw_rev_3-0_spreads.pdf>.

De Propris, Lisa, and Hypponen, Laura. "Creative Clusters and Governance: The Dominance of the Hollywood Film Cluster". *Creative Cities, Cultural Clusters and Local Development*. Ed. Philip Cooke and Luciana Lazzeretti. Cheltenham: Edward Elgar, 2008. 340–371.

Evans Graeme. "Creative Cities, Creative Spaces and Urban Policy." *Urban Studies*. 46.5&6 (2009): 1003–1040.

Florida L Richard. *The Rise of the Creative Class: And How Its Transforming Work, Leisure, Community and Everyday Life*. New York: Basic Books, 2002.

Harvey, Adrian. *Funding Arts and Culture in a Time of Austerity. Arts Council England*. London: New Local Government Network. 2016. Web. 1 Feb. 2016. <http://www.nlgn.org.uk/public/wp-content/uploads/Funding-Arts-and-Culture.pdf>.

Kozinets V Robert, and Netnography Redefined. *Netnography Redefined*. 2nd ed. London: Sage, 2015.

Landry Charles. *The Creative City: A Toolkit for Urban Innovators*. New York: Routledge, 2000.

Li, Yaojun. Economist. *Breaking Out*. 21 Feb. 2015. Web. 1 Sep. 2015. <http://www.economist.com/news/britain/21644155-britain-bangladeshis-have-overtaken-pakistanis-credit-poor-job-market-when-they-arrived>.

Lymperopoulou, Kitty. Still Disadvantaged? The Educational Attainment of Ethnic Minority Groups. Filed Under: Ethnicity. *Manchester Policy Blogs*. Manchester University. 14 May 2015. Web. 1 Sep. 2015. <http://blog.policy.manchester.ac.uk/featured/2015/05/still-disadvantaged-the-educational-attainment-of-ethnic-minority-groups/>.

Mommaas, Hans. "Spaces of Culture and Economy: Mapping the Cultural-creative Cluster Landscape." *Creative Economies, Creative Cities: Asian-European Perspectives*. Ed. Lily Kong and Justin O'Connor. Netherlands: Springer, 2009. 45–59.

Nichols-Clarke Terry, ed. *The City as Entertainment Machine*. Oxford: Elsevier, 2004.
Oitij-jo. *Business Plan 2015–2017*. Sep. 2015. Unpublished.
Oitij-jo. Website. 2013. Web. 1 Sep. 2015. <www.oitijjo.org>.
ONS. *Ethnicity & Labour Market, 2011 Census for England & Wales Poverty: Low income & ethnicity*. 13 Nov. 2014. Web. 1 Sep. 2015. <http://www.poverty.org.uk/06/index.shtml>.
Porter, Micheal. *The Competitive Advantage of Nations, Harvard Business Review*. 1990. Mar.–Apr. issue. Web. 24 Aug. 2015. <https://hbr.org/1990/03/the-competitive-advantage-of-nations>.
Pratt, C. Andy. "Policy Transfer and the Field of the Cultural and Creative Industries: Learning from Europe? Creative Economies, Creative Cities: Asian European Perspectives." *Creative Economies, Creative Cities: Asian-European Perspectives*. Ed. Lily Kong and Justin O'Connor. Heidelberg: Springer, 2009. 9–23.
Radjou Navi, Jaideep Prabhu, and Simone Ahuja. *Jugaad Innovation: Think Frugal, Be Flexible, Generate Breakthrough Growth*. New York: John Wiley Sons Inc, 2012.
Saxena B. Sanchita. *Made in Bangladesh, Cambodia and Sri Lanka: The Labor Behind the Global Garments and Textiles Industries*. Amhurst, NY: Cambria Press, 2014.
Somerville Will, Dhananjayan Sriskandarajah, and Maria Latorre. *A Reluctant Country of Immigration*. 21 Jul. 2009. UK: Migration Information Source, 2009.
Stokes Kathleen, Emma Clarence, Lauren Anderson, and April Rinne. *Making Sense of the UK Collaborative Economy*. London: Nesta UK Collaborative Lab, 2014.
United Nations Conference on Trade and Development. *Creative Industries and Development*. Eleventh session. São Paulo, 13–18 June 2004. Web. 1. Sep. 2015. <http://unctad.org/en/docs/tdxibpd13_en.pdf>.
Visram Rozina. *Asians in Britain*. 2nd ed. London: Pluto Press, 2002.
Visram Rozina. *Ayahs, Lascars and Princes: Indians in Britain: 1700–1947*. London: Pluto Press, 1986.

What 'value' South Asian arts in Britain?

Jasjit Singh

ABSTRACT
This article examines the historical and contemporary articulation of the 'value' of South Asian Arts in Britain. Having examined the development of minority arts in Britain and in particular 'South Asian Arts', I examine how South Asian arts organisations have presented the 'cultural value' of these arts to funders and participants. Taking 'cultural value' to refer to the value associated with engaging with and participating in art and culture (Crossick and Kaszynska, 13) this article examines how South Asian arts in the British cultural and creative industries have been impacted by the 'value' agenda. I find that even though South Asian arts forms play an important role in enabling audiences who may rarely engage with the cultural industries to participate in relevant arts, South Asian arts organisations continue to be required to articulate their value primarily as part of a commitment to 'diversity'.

Introduction

On 6 June 2014, the then Culture Secretary Sajid Javid, reflected on some of his cultural experiences growing up as a British Pakistani, and of the impact of a visit to the cinema as a six-year old to watch the Bollywood blockbuster Sholay, an experience which left him 'transfixed by this amazing spectacle unfolding on the big screen'. In this very first speech as Culture Secretary Javid went on to reflect that 'adults from black and minority ethnic backgrounds are significantly less engaged with the arts than their white counterparts ... [and are] much less likely to attend a performance or visit a gallery'. He further noted that the fact that BME applicants were awarded just 5.5% of Grants for the Arts awards in 2013 despite making up 14% of the UK's population highlighted a lack of engagement by those from BME backgrounds with the arts. Reflecting on some of the reasons behind this lack of engagement he wondered if there were sufficient numbers of visible role models, if talent is being developed in the right way, and if the cultural and creative industries in Britain make enough of an effort to reach out to ethnic minority communities.

This article examines how minority arts, in particular 'South Asian Arts' have developed in Britain, and how South Asian arts organisations have presented the 'cultural value' of these arts to funders and participants. Taking Crossick and Kaszynska's (13) definition of 'cultural value' as the value associated with engaging with and participating in art and culture where 'culture' includes 'theatre and dance; film; visual arts; photography; literature; storytelling; music; monuments and murals, as well as museums, archives, tangible and intangible heritage, and more' this article examines how South Asian arts in the British cultural and creative industries have been impacted by the 'value' agenda. The aim is to critically understand how 'South Asian Arts' have been valued by state actors and by participants themselves. Both community art making and publically funded art are explored, using data collected through structured literature searches and a small online survey.

The literature search was structured around four areas; (a) reports and research produced by funding bodies; (b) annual reports and ephemera produced by South Asian Arts organisations; (c) magazines regularly publishing articles relating to South Asian Arts and (d) academic research. Alongside this, an online survey was developed and implemented. The survey was advertised through social media and through the various networks created by the above engagement. As well as asking questions about the different types of minority ethnic events which participants engaged in, questions were asked about how they valued this engagement. The survey ran for two months between May and June 2014 and in total gathered 32 responses, 11 male and 21 female between the ages of 19 and 56. Where relevant, quotations from the survey will be included in the analysis.

'Ethnic Minority arts'

The publication of Naseem Khan's highly influential 'The Arts Britain Ignores' in 1976 signalled the first discussion of the place of 'ethnic minority arts' which she described as 'an energetic but struggling sub-culture … which exists for the communities alone' (5). Khan (6) argued that a separate funding allocation for 'ethnic minority arts' was necessary in order to:

(1) allow 'coloured children' to learn positive aspects of what is 'commonly counted a disadvantage'
(2) encourage different types of arts
(3) provide new influences and experiences for those living in Britain, as ethnic arts could be 'a possible source of enjoyment for all' (Khan 7).

Public funding for 'ethnic minority arts' emerged following the civil uprisings in the 1980s in Brixton, leading to the development of the Arts Council's Ethnic Minorities Action Plan (Malik 18).[1] As Malik (19) explains, the role of local councils particularly the Greater London Council's (GLC) Ethnic Minority Arts Committee was significant at this time in boosting minority cultural activities. At the time 'South Asian arts' were included in the 'ethnic minority arts' and 'Black arts' categories. Although there were moves to promote 'South Asian arts' as a distinct category throughout the 1980s and 1990s, this led many South Asian artists to feel that they were categorised by race or ethnicity often placing them in a 'straightjacket of conformity', crippling artistic creativity and confining them to a limited range of themes (Fisher 63).

For Hylton (40) this labelling of artists as 'South Asian' was a direct consequence of Khan's report which had conveyed a notion of a self-referencing field of 'ethnic arts' leading funding initiatives to support 'cultural diversity' which implied that normality was white and everything else 'diverse' (23). In 2011, in response to these criticisms and part fuelled by the Equality Act 2010, the Arts Council presented a 'Creative case' for diversity which presented diversity and equality as important factors which helped 'sustain, refresh, replenish and release the true potential of England's artistic talent, regardless of people's background' (Arts Council "What is the Creative Case for Diversity" 3). The distinction between 'mainstream' and 'diverse' art forms remains however. As this article will demonstrate, the development of South Asian arts in Britain continues to maintain this division as 'diverse' art forms remain outside the 'mainstream'.

A typology of 'South Asian arts'

As outlined above, Khan did not use 'South Asian arts' as a distinct category, rather she wrote about 'ethnic minority arts' which included Bangladeshi, Indian and Pakistani arts. By 1994 however, Farrell found the term 'South Asian' being 'used widely in the context of arts to mean styles of music, dance and visual arts from the Indian sub-continent, i.e. from Bangladesh, Pakistan, India and Sri Lanka' (1). For Meduri, this change occurred during the 1980s as arts officers, academics, venue managers and funding agencies rechristened Indian forms as South Asian forms (299) turning the label 'South Asian' into a dominant institutional category as major dance organisations including Akademi, Kadam and Sampad, funded by the Arts Council began to use the area studies label to promote Bharatanatyam, Kathak and Odissi (Meduri "Labels, Histories, Politics" 224).

A number of distinctions can be made between different types of 'South Asian arts', one being between Marghi and Desi traditions. Marghi (lit 'on the path') traditions are highly formalised, often based on ancient texts and are passed down from a Guru (teacher) to a shishya (student) whereas Desi arts are more localised traditions which develop in local contexts. A similar distinction is described by Farrell et al. (117) who explains that for South Asian music 'a conceptual divide has long existed between classical and folk music ... expressed by the terms shastriya sangit (classical) and lok sangit (folk)'. In terms of desi traditions which have evolved in Britain, by far the most popular is that of Bhangra, which emerged in the mid-1980s (Banerji 1988; Baumann 1990; Bennett 1997; Dudrah "Drum'n'dhol: British bhangra music" 2002) developing a number of 'regional' identities in association with different music scenes and local South Asian communities in British cities; for example, in Southall, London (Baumann 1990: 83), the midlands city of Birmingham (Dudrah "Bhangra: Birmingham and Beyond" 2007) or the north-eastern city of Newcastle (Bennett 1997; 110). It is important to note that these categories are open to interpretation with Iyer (7) viewing classical styles of South Asian dance such as Bharatnatyam as a 'marghi' art forms and British South Asian dance as a 'desi' art form.

South Asian arts organisations in Britain

The history of South Asian arts organisations in Britain begins with the establishment in the 1970s of community-specific, culture-focused institutions including the first overseas branch of the Bharatiya Vidhya Bhavan in London in 1972. By the 1980s a number of South Asian dance organisations had emerged in response to state funding opportunities including Akademi (established in 1979 as the Academy of Indian Dance), SAMPAD (established in 1990 in Birmingham), AdiTi a national organisation for South Asian dance in Britain (established in 1989 and now dissolved) and Kadam, a Bedford based development agency for South Asian dance (established in 1990). Alongside these South Asian music and dance organisations, a number of British South Asian theatre organisations were established from the 1970s onwards including Tara Arts, Tamasha and the Kali Theatre Company (Hingorani 2010). Many of these organisations were awarded funding in 2014 as designated Arts Council 'National Portfolio Organisations':

Name	Location	Established	Discipline
Akademi	Camden, London	1979	Dance
Akram Khan Dance	Islington, London	2000	Dance
Art Asia	Southampton	1981	Theatre
Asian Arts Agency	Bristol	1997	Combined Arts
Bharatiya Vidya Bhavan	Hammersmith, London	1972	Music
Darbar Arts Culture and Heritage Trust	Leicester	2005	Music
Gem Arts	Gateshead	1989	Combined Arts
Kala Sangam	Bradford	1993	Combined Arts
Kali Theatre Company	Lewisham	1991	Theatre
Milapfest	Liverpool	1985	Combined Arts
Peshkar Productions	Oldham	1991	Combined Arts
Rifco Arts	Watford	1999	Theatre
Sampad	Birmingham	1990	Combined Arts
Shobana Jeyasingh Dance Company	Islington (London)	1988	Dance
Sonia Sabri Company	Birmingham	2002	Dance
South Asian Arts	Leeds	1997	Music
Tamasha Theatre Company Ltd	Tower Hamlets	1989	Theatre
Tara	Wandsworth	1977	Theatre

Clarke and Hodgson (7) distinguish between these 'public facing' organisations and 'community facing' South Asian arts organisations. They define 'public facing' organisations as those which are funded principally by public money and/or sponsorship, are accountable to public bodies (e.g. local authorities, funding councils) and are not bound to the communities with which they engage and serve. In contrast, 'community facing' organisations are usually privately funded by individuals. These 'community facing' organisations are focused on the cultural needs or aspirations of a particular community where making connections with other communities is not necessarily a priority. As a consequence of funding requirements it is clear that these different types of South Asian arts organisations engage with the 'diversity' agenda in very different ways.

Examining the types of South Asian arts offered by the 'public facing' South Asian arts organisations, it appears that the 'Marghi' (classical) forms are more commonly offered than the 'Desi' (folk) art forms. In this regard, a particular type of South Asian heritage is being funded, produced and re-produced in and through the cultural industries in Britain in which 'classical' art forms including theatre, music and dance are often privileged above folk art forms. These types of art forms are part of the authorised heritage discourse (AHD) 'a professional discourse that tends to dominate national and international Western debates about the nature, value and meaning of heritage' (Smith 2012: 162). In order to ensure their recognition by the state and to obtain funding, many South Asian arts organisations know they must focus on art forms which are part of the AHD while emphasising the 'cultural value' of their offer to a diverse set of participants. I now examine how South Asian arts organisations in Britain have presented the 'cultural value' of these arts, using four themes outlined by the Arts Council (2014) focusing on their economic value, their benefit to health and well-being, their impact on society and their role in education.

Economic value

In terms of attracting visitors, by far the largest South Asian arts events held in Britain are the annual summer Melas with Birmingham attracting 125,000 visitors in its first year, London attracting an audience of over 80,000 and Manchester attracting over 60,000 attendees.[2] Originally celebrations of 'South Asian culture', Melas are now recognised as multi-arts festivals drawing in huge crowds from diverse communities (Qureshi 96).[3] In their study of the economic and social impact of eleven festivals in the East Midlands, Maughan and Bianchini (2004) included the Leicester Belgrave Mela, a two day Asian cultural and social event established in 1983. Of the eleven festivals examined, they found the Leicester Mela attracting the largest overall audience with approximately 100,000 attendees (4). They observed a clear link between ethnicity and attendance as most non-white festival goers only attended the Leicester Belgrave Mela and the Derby Caribbean Carnival. Including these two festivals they found that Asian or Asian British ethnic groups made up 11.2% of audiences, whereas excluding these festivals the Asian percentage declined to 1.4% suggesting 'a strong need for festivals to broaden their appeal to Asian and Black audiences' (2004: 9). The appeal of Melas to diverse audiences is also evidenced by the non-mainstream sponsors they attract[4] and by the opportunities they provide to health practitioners to engage with diverse groups on issues relating to health and well-being.

As well as assisting in the organisation of Melas, 'public facing' South Asian arts organisations regularly contribute to local cultural provision.[5] The influence of these established South Asian arts organisations also filters across into communities with smaller South Asian populations with the Asian Art Agency based in Bristol for instance helping South Asian communities in Swindon and Plymouth.[6]

Conversely, many of the events organised by 'community facing' organisations are relatively hidden, often advertised within community networks and usually taking place in venues owned or run by members of minority ethnic communities including religious institutions and cultural centres. Consequently there has been little research into their economic impact. Although Voluntary Arts England estimate that there were 49,000 grass roots or amateur arts organisations in England in 2009 often run by unpaid staff (Ramsden et al. 2011) it is unlikely that this number includes South Asian community facing organisations which although providing grassroots arts, rarely label themselves specifically as arts organisations.

Health and well-being

In a 2014 report, the Arts Council reported that 'participants are attracted to and demonstrate higher levels of commitment to activities that are culturally relevant to them' (30). Indeed, both 'public facing'[7] and 'community facing'[8] South Asian arts organisations provide a number of such 'culturally relevant' activities to improve the health and well-being of those who may not otherwise engage in arts activities. Many of these activities are more readily accessible to South Asians who may not have a strong command of English and who may not feel confident to engage with health professionals. It is clear therefore that for some British South Asians, culturally specific South Asian events can act as a catalyst to engage in ways to improve their health and well-being.

Societal value

Research into South Asian communities has highlighted the role the arts and music can play as markers of collective identity and in challenging common perceptions (Um 2006, Clarke and Hodgson 2012). For Clarke and Hodgson (2) South Asian music and the arts can 'represent further different places from which multiculturalism might be experienced and understood'. This in turn could help individuals and communities to articulate their identities, to experience and affirm their cultures, to raise the profile of their cultures to wider audiences and to promote or affirm cultural confidence which may also improve cultural well-being (7). According to Nagle (157) the need for members of minority groups to be able to affirm cultural confidence comes from the fact that multicultural policy has left many second-generation youth 'marginalized in society and lacking the self-esteem required to build bridges with other groups'. Indeed, it was suggested following the 'race riots' of the 1980s that if young members of minority groups could gain greater awareness of their 'ethnic heritage' as well as the cultures of other groups they would gain greater confidence in their identity negating the need to turn to violence in order to express themselves (Nagle 156–157).

Many of the online survey respondents highlighted the importance of their ethnic heritage with a 23-year-old female from Leeds stating that it gave her 'a sense of grounding, belonging, identity and confidence', a 41-year-old female from Leicester viewing it as something which 'defines you as a person … gives you your identity and sense of belonging' and a 19-year-old male from Bradford explaining how connecting 'with the culture, values and knowledge of my ancestors is equally as important as learning the ones in the place I am born'.

Respondents also highlighted how participation in South Asian arts had played an important role in building their self-esteem and self-confidence, with a 35-year-old white female from Wolverhampton explaining how she had 'made new friends, learned about another culture, increased my confidence and learned new skills' through her participation in Kathak. A 20-year-old female from Birmingham felt that participation in South Asian arts had helped her 'to understand my place in a diasporic South Asian community'.

Engagement in South Asian arts may also encourage members of BME communities to pursue careers in the arts/creative industries, an area in which they are severely underrepresented.[9] A 23-year-old female from Leeds explained that she wanted 'to be involved in the creative industries, especially arts, heritage and culture and preferably with a focus on South Asia'. In filling gaps created by the absence of South Asian literature and music in mainstream British society and in school curricula Prickett (2004) argues that South Asian arts offer potential for a more comprehensive understanding of Britain's multicultural foundations. Participation in South Asian arts can also strengthen social relations and interactions, with melas for instance 'drawing in multiple, diverse and intergenerational communities … within a shared atmosphere of celebration' (Qureshi 7).

For Hingorani (191) South Asian theatre plays an important role in postcolonial Britain as it inscribes 'difference' on the British stage while also contesting homogeneous constructions of national cultural identity. South Asian arts exhibitions can also challenge stereotypes, as Hashmi and Poovaya-Smith explain regarding the 'Intelligent Rebellion: Women Artists of Pakistan exhibition' which they curated in 1985. They explain how this exhibition overturned 'a number of stereotypes that the West may have, about contemporary art practised in a Muslim country' (Hashmi and Poovaya-Smith 1997).

In their examination of participation in local authority arts events by the South Asian community in Blackburn, Syson and Wood (246) again found a link between ethnicity and participation in the arts. It is probable that any reported high level of engagement in the arts by members of minority communities mostly takes place with minority ethnic arts and in venues away from the mainstream.[10] Examples include 'Kavi Darbars' (poetry symposiums) which are regularly organised in community venues across the country including Nottingham, Hounslow, Derby and Kent[11] with little funding from the state. That these arts events are organised by 'community facing' organisations has important implications for the study of these communities and cultural value more generally.

Education

Many 'public facing' South Asian arts organisations highlight the role that South Asian arts can play in educating wider society in South Asian art forms and in encouraging the public 'to reassess and challenge its view of South Asian dance and preconceptions of South Asia as a whole'.[12] As well as presenting South Asian arts to the general public a number of these organisations also work with schools, with Clarke and Hodgson (2012: 13) noting how Saarang's work with primary schools in Newcastle brings 'experiences of South Asian and other world cultures to largely ethnically unmixed areas such as rural County Durham'. Learning South Asian arts also facilitates new experiences with Clarke and Hodgson describing how the predominantly white students of Hindustani classical music at Newcastle University learning from expert Indian musicians 'has meant an encounter with another culture grounded in a lived relationship with their teachers' (14). Indeed, students of any background who learn Marghi traditions through the guru-disciple tradition are opening themselves up to new educational experiences as learning to play Indian classical musical instruments for instance would traditionally only have been open to members of musical families.[13]

Learning South Asian arts can also act as an important method of religious and cultural transmission, with David (90) finding Bharatanatyam classes being used by British Gujaratis and Tamils to teach their children about Indian culture.[14] In Leeds, SAA-UK have implemented classes to teach Sikh women traditional wedding songs which would otherwise have been passed down from generation to generation but which have somehow become lost in the frantic process of migration in the 1960s and 1970s.[15]

As formal structures have not yet been developed for the teaching of Indian classical music in Britain Farrell et al. (117) note that amongst second and third-generation South Asian musicians in Britain knowledge of, or training in, classical music is not the norm and therefore 'musical learning takes place at the interface of a number of formal and informal learning situations: within the community, at religious worship, in schools, colleges and adult education centres, in clubs and recording studios'. (Farrell et al. 117). An important role which South Asian arts organisations can play is to equip South Asian artists with the skills they need to break in to the mainstream, or to become role models and teachers for younger artists.[16]

Conclusions

This article has shown that the place of South Asian arts in the creative industries in Britain has changed over the years from being promoted as 'community based' art forms which allow members of minority communities to engage with positive aspects of their culture to the current position where South Asian arts organisations are promoted as being valuable to wider society as they contribute economically and also provide a number of societal, health and education benefits. The imposition of labels for minority art forms has also been highlighted as an issue of concern for those participating, with these labels often being imposed by funders and policy makers. The term 'South Asian arts' for instance has been shown to refer primarily to art forms of Indian origin even as South Asian arts organisations develop ways of engaging with and promoting art forms which appeal to those from non-South Asian backgrounds.

The role of different types of South Asian arts organisations in the creative industries has also been examined with 'public facing' organisations providing opportunities for people of all backgrounds to learn about particular types of South Asian arts while also opening these up to new audiences. Examining the cultural value of South Asian arts using the four measures of their impact on the economy, on health and well-being, on society and on education has highlighted that these arts can play an important role in engaging those who might be less likely to participate in arts activities. Whereas it has been shown that some South Asian artists may not wish to be pigeonholed as purely 'South Asian', others wish to engage with South Asian arts because it provides them with a link to their heritage. 'Community facing' South Asian arts organisations also play an important role in organising events which may not be labelled as arts events but which play an important role for those South Asians who may not feel comfortable in engaging in more mainstream events.

Despite funders, journalists and politicians regularly raising the issue of the lack of diversity and BME engagement in the arts, minority arts in general and 'South Asian arts' in particular continuously struggle to find a space in the mainstream. Many of the publically funded South Asian arts organisations are compelled to articulate their 'cultural value' as part of a commitment to 'diversity'. For Berrey (2015) however, the notion of 'diversity' actually hinders conversations about underlying issues such as racial inequality. Is diversity in the arts seen as a positive for the reason that it opens up the possibilities for established 'mainstream' arts organisations to engage with hard to reach groups? Although as this article has shown, South Asian arts forms and organisations play a number of important roles for a variety of different audiences, in terms of their 'cultural value', over 40 years after Naseem Khan's report, they are rarely regarded as being part of the 'mainstream'.

Notes

1. Before this, during the late 1970s and early 1980s diasporic dance forms were disseminated through 'grass-roots amateur practices in local community halls, temples and specialist venues such as London's Bharatiya Vidya Bhavan' (Prickett 6).
2. These details can be found at Birmingham (http://www.birminghammela.com/about-birmingham-mela/), London (http://www.londonmela.org/), Manchester (http://www.manchester.gov.uk/news/article/6388/manchester_mega_mela_returns_to_manchester) and Southampton (http://artasia.org.uk/highlight-6/) – all accessed June 5 2014.

3. Although as Hodgson (2013: 208) found these events need to ensure that they reflect a variety of diverse traditions in order to maintain their appeal or risk becoming 'mono-cultural' as in the case of the Bradford mela between 2009/2010.
4. Details of past and current mela sponsors including including KTC, Savera, Noon Products, Rubicon, Supermalt, Western Union, Pataks, Sharwoods, East End Foods, Tilda, Sahara, British Airways, Kingfisher, Cobra, Khukuri, Virgin Media, Zee TV and Sony TV Asia, companies which would rarely invest in more mainstream arts can be found at http://www.londonmela.org/sponsorship/ and http://www.manchestermela.co.uk/sponsors.htm – both accessed June 5 2014.
5. The study of the Economic value of Birmingham's cultural sector and the examination of The Creative & Digital Industries in Leeds for instance provide little data on how South Asian Arts specifically contribute to local economies.
6. Another example is Shisha's ArtSouthAsia project, the first international programme of visual culture from Bangladesh, India, Pakistan and Sri Lanka in July 2002 led to 'the North West cities of Oldham, Preston, Liverpool and Manchester … [seeing] significant events and exhibitions curated by individuals from each of the contributing countries' (Holt and Turney 338).
7. Programmes organised by 'public facing' organisations include SAA-UK's 'Khushi project' and Kala Sangam's 'Kala Sukoon' focusing on mental health problems in the South Asian community in Yorkshire. Sampad's Antenatal Music and Movement project for Asian women (Arts Council "Arts, Health and Wellbeing" 38) ran over 18 months during 2001 and 2002 in areas of Birmingham and Walsall where there was a low uptake of antenatal care from women from 'more closed Asian communities … [where] English is often a second language and there is resistance to attending any classes for preparation for birth, and also a high infant mortality rate amongst non-English speakers' (Durdey 2006).
8. Examples include the work of the Pakistan Cultural Society (PCS) in Newcastle who started a twice-weekly well-being group to sensitively address 'real issues' affecting the Asian community by delivering a physical and educational programme to help combat such health conditions as obesity, depression, cholesterol problems and heart disease (http://www.ethnicnow.com/lifestyle/health-lifestyle/community-wellbeing-project-proves-to-be-a-life-changing-experience-for-north-east-women/ – accessed July 8 2014).
9. A recent report highlighted how despite over 50% of Londoners coming from a BAME background, the proportion of people from non-white backgrounds working in the creative industries is half of what it is across the rest of the economy. For further details, see: http://creativediversitynetwork.com/resource/a-strategy-for-change/ – accessed May 19 2014.
10. The issue of a lack of BME engagement in the arts does not appear to have gone away. In a presentation at a conference on The Creative Case for Diversity in Britain (2011), Dr. Victoria Walsh critiqued many of the initiatives which have been undertaken by the cultural sector and noted that 'despite over a decade of substantial dedicated funding and activity framed by policies of 'cultural diversity' no significant increase in visits to the art museum by 'minority' audiences had been realised'.
11. Further details about the Kavi Darbars can be found here: http://www.nottinghampost.com/Recitals-talks-poetry-event/story-19720780-detail/story.html (Nottingham), http://www.sgss.org/Newsreel.aspx?month=4&year=2012 (Hounslow), http://www.writingeastmidlands.co.uk/events/kavi-darbar-poetry-evening/ (Derby), https://www.youtube.com/watch?v=p0Xi-KiTAMc (Kent) – all accessed June 15 2014.
12. See Akademi's Annual report from 2013 available at: http://apps.charitycommission.gov.uk/Accounts/Ends49%5C0001107249_AC_20130331_E_C.pdf – accessed May 18 2014. Also the SAA-UK annual report highlights the role played by South Asian arts organisations in exposing those who have not encountered South Asian arts before to new art forms with one attendee explaining 'this was my first Indian Classical Music concert' SAA-UK Annual Report 2007/08, page 13. Available at: http://www.saa-uk.org/documents/Annual_Report_2007-08.pdf – accessed May 18 2014.

13. For example, Roopa Panesar an internationally renowned sitar player 'admits her family background is very different to many Indian musicians, where musicianship often runs in families and famous dynasties go back decades and even centuries'. For further details, see: http://www.mancunianmatters.co.uk/content/0806622-you-know-sitar-now-meet-rest-indian-classical-music-uk – accessed June 11 2014.
14. Katrak (5) argues these learning these dance forms are also a way to 'inculcate and instil certain traditional values about womanhood and the conventionally acceptable roles of wife and mother'.
15. For further details, see: http://www.saa-uk.org/education_indianfolk.php – accessed July 5 2014.
16. For instance Jasdeep Singh Degun from Leeds who has performed in a number of high profile and has also collaborated with many orchestras such as the National Youth Orchestra and Aldeburgh Young Musicians and also took part in a BBC2 Documentary and performed at Buckingham Palace for HRH Prince Harry as part of Goldie's Band (http://www.saa-uk.org/artist/jasdeep-degun). He recently performed as part of the BBC Proms at the Royal Albert Hall: https://www.soas.ac.uk/news/newsitem93970.html

Disclosure statement

No potential conflict of interest was reported by the author.

References

Arts Council. *Arts, Health and Wellbeing*. 2007. Web. 05 Mar. 2014. <http://www.artscouncil.org.uk/media/uploads/phpC1AcLv.pdf>.
Arts Council. *What is the Creative Case for Diversity*. 2011. <http://www.artscouncil.org.uk/media/uploads/pdf/What_is_the_Creative_Case_for_Diversity.pdf>.
Arts Council. *The Value of Arts and Culture to People and Society – An Evidence Review*. 2014. <http://www.artscouncil.org.uk/what-we-do/research-and-data/value-arts-and-culture-people-and-society-evidence-review/>.
Banerji S. "From Ghazals to Bhangra in Great Britain." *Popular Music* 7 (1988): 207–14.
Banerji S., and G. Baumann. "Bhangra 1984–8: Fusion and Professionalisation in a Genre of South Asian Dance Music." *Black Music in Britain: Essays on the Afro-Asian Contribution to Popular Music*. Ed. P. Oliver. Milton Keynes: Open University Press, 1990.
Baumann G. "The Re-Invention of Bhangra: Social Change and Aesthetic Shifts in a Punjabi Music in Britain." *The World of Music* 32.2 (1990): 81–97.
Bennett A. "Bhangra in Newcastle: Music, Ethnic Identity and the Role of Local Knowledge." *Innovation: The European Journal of the Social Sciences* 10.1 (1997): 107–16.
Berrey, E. 2015. "Diversity is for White People: The Big Lie Behind a Well-intended Word." Salon. Accessed October 24, 2016. http://www.salon.com/2015/10/26/diversity_is_for_white_people_the_big_lie_behind_a_well_intended_word/
Clarke, D., and T. Hodgson. *Connecting Cultures? South Asian Musics and an Emerging Multiculturalism in North East England*. AHRC Connected Communities, 2012. <http://research.ncl.ac.uk/media/sites/researchwebsites/icmus/South%20Asian%20Musics%20in%20Newcastle%20and%20the%20North%20East.pdf>.

Crossick, G., and P. Kaszynska. *Understanding the Value of Arts & Culture: The AHRC Cultural Value Project*. 2015. <http://www.ahrc.ac.uk/documents/publications/cultural-value-project-final-report/>.

David A. "Negotiating Identity: Dance and Religion in British Hindu Communities." 2009. *Dance Matters: Performing India on Local and Global Stages*. Ed. P. Chakravorty and N. Gupta. New Delhi: Routledge, 2012. 89–107.

Durdey, T. *Dance: Creating Wellbeing through Movement and Dance Conference Report*. 2006. <http://www.ahsw.org.uk/userfiles/Other_Resources/Performing_Arts/Dance%20CONF%20REPORT.pdf>.

Farrell G. *South Asian Music Teaching in Change*. London: David Fulton Publishers, 1994.

Farrell, G., G. Welch, and J. Bhowmick. "South Asian Music in Britain." 2006. *Diasporas and Interculturalism in Asian Performing Arts: Translating Traditions*. Ed. H. Um. London: Routledge, 2004. 104–128.

Fisher, J. "Cultural Diversity and Institutional Policy." 2010. *Beyond Cultural Diversity: The Case for Creativity*, 1st ed. Ed. R. Appignanesi. London: Third Text Publications, 2010. 61–70.

Hashmi S., and N. Poovaya-Smith. *The Draped & the Shaped: Textiles and Costumes from Pakistan*. Bradford: Bradford, City of, Metropolitan Council, Arts, Museums & Libraries Division, 1997.

Hingorani D. *British Asian Theatre: Dramaturgy, Process and Performance*. London: Palgrave, 2010.

Hodgson T. E. "Multicultural Harmony? Pakistani Muslims and Music in Bradford". 2013. *Music, Culture and Identity in the Muslim World: Performance, Politics and Piety*. Ed. K. Salhi. London: Routledge, 2013.

Holt J., and L. Turney. "The Singular Journey: South Asian Visual Art in Britain." *A Postcolonial People: South Asians in Britain*. Ed. S. Sayyid, N. Ali and V. S. Kalra. 2006. 329–338.

Hylton R. *The Nature of the Beast: Cultural Diversity and the Visual Arts Sector – A Study of Policies, Initiatives and Attitudes 1976-2006*. Bath: Institute of Contemporary Interdisciplinary Arts, 2007.

Iyer A. *South Asian Dance: The British Experience*. Routledge, 1997.

Katrak K. "'Cultural Translation' of Bharata Natyam into 'Contemporary Indian Dance': Second-Generation South Asian Americans and Cultural Politics in Diasporic Locations." *South Asian Popular Culture* 2.2 (2004): 79–102.

Khan N. *The Arts Britain Ignores*. London: Commission for Racial Equality, 1976.

Malik S. *Representing Black Britain: Black and Asian Images on Television*. Thousand Oaks, CA: Sage, 2001.

Meduri A. "The Transfiguration of Indian/Asian Dance in the United Kingdom: Contemporary Bharatanatyam in Global Contexts." *Asian Theatre Journal* 25 (2008a): 298–328.

Meduri A. "Labels, Histories, Politics: Indian/South Asian Dance on the Global Stage." *Dance Research* 26 (2008b): 223–243.

Nagle D. J. *Multiculturalism's Double-Bind: Creating Inclusivity, Cosmopolitanism and Difference*. Ashgate Publishing, 2012.

Prickett S. "Techniques and Institutions: The Transformation of British Dance Tradition through South Asian Dance." *Dance Research* 22 (2004): 1–21.

Qureshi I. *Coming of Age: Celebrating 21 Years of Mela in the UK*. Bradford: 2010.

Ramsden H., et al. *The Role of Grass Roots Activities in Communities: A Scoping Study*. Third Sector Research Centre (TRSC), 2011. <http://www.birmingham.ac.uk/generic/tsrc/documents/tsrc/working-papers/working-paper-68.pdf>..

Syson, F., and H. Wood. "Local Authority Arts Events and the South Asian Community: Unmet Needs – A UK Case Study." *Managing Leisure* 11 (2006): 245–258.

Um H.-K. *Diasporas and Interculturalism in Asian Performing Arts: Translating Traditions*. London: Taylor & Francis, 2006.

The production of *Ek Tha Tiger*: A marriage of convenience between Bollywood and the Irish film and tourist industries

Giovanna Rampazzo

ABSTRACT

This article examines a collaboration between the Irish and Hindi film industries, adopting the production of Kabir Khan's *Ek Tha Tiger* (2012) in Dublin as a case study. It critically narrates the arc of the film's production, foregrounding the intersecting concerns of Yash Raj Films and Irish creative and cultural institutions. *Ek Tha Tiger* represents Ireland through constructed idyllic images which proved to be successful in attracting tourists. Tracing the links between the production of the film and the promotion of tourism to Ireland, this article explains how the film was used to construct a 'tourist gaze' for audiences in a process reminiscent of Foucault's notions of the power of surveillance (See "Discipline and Punish" and "Power/Knowledge") as it acts through institutions of tourism. Drawing on participant observation in the film's production, alongside interviews with the film's producers and representatives of Irish institutions, the discussion explores how transnational marketing strategies influenced the production of *Ek Tha Tiger*.

Introduction

Ek Tha Tiger (Once There was a Tiger; 2012), directed by Kabir Khan and produced by Aditya Chopra of the renowned Indian production company Yash Raj Films, is to date the first big budget Bollywood film to make extensive use of an Irish urban location. While the film was shot in several other countries including India, Turkey, Cuba and Thailand, a critical component of its storyline is set in Dublin. This article critically narrates the arc of the film's production, demonstrating how the genesis of the film is linked with national policies and strategies aimed at attracting tourism and investments to Ireland through film. Foregrounding the connections between the making of *Ek Tha Tiger* and the advertisement of Ireland as a tourist destination, this article outlines how the showcasing of institutionally constructed images of Dublin resulted in the creation of a 'tourist gaze' for prospective spectators and potential tourists, which can arguably be described as an organised and controlled mode of viewing comparable to Foucault's 'medical gaze' (17). In so doing, the author argues that by promoting and cultivating the anticipation of a collective viewing experience of a country or in this case, an Irish urban location, cinematic representations can be mobilised in the service of 'cultural tourism', resulting in the creation of simplified, stereotyped and spectacular imagery constructions. Such images actually provide only a partial view of Irish culture and society, erasing its complexities and limiting the viewers' knowledge of Ireland to only few salient dimensions presented as if they were the whole picture. Additionally, this article expands on the way Trinity College Dublin, Ireland's oldest and most reputable university, significantly featured in the film, strategically used *Ek Tha Tiger* to raise its profile among prospective Indian students. This discussion also refers to insights from Freeman's stakeholder theory which acknowledges that organisations should be managed in the interest of all their stakeholders in order to succeed (Freeman, 25). Significantly, the following exploration foregrounds the intersecting concerns between the production of *Ek Tha Tiger* and Irish cultural and national institutions, which benefited from the choice of Dublin as a location for the film.

Methodology

The filming of *Ek Tha Tiger* in Dublin occurred over five weeks between 10 September and 14 October 2011. During this period, participant observation was conducted by working on set as a film extra and as a location trainee, and by observing the filming along with crowds of Bollywood fans gathered around the sets. Additionally, interviews were conducted with audience members, representatives of the *Ek Tha Tiger* production team, Trinity College Dublin and Yash Raj Films executives, and the Irish Film Commissioner. A case study approach was employed in the examination of the production of the film, since, according to Creswell such a research method allows the exploration and understanding of complex social phenomena, providing holistic and in-depth explanations of the events in question (186). Yin further argues that 'a case study investigates a contemporary phenomenon (the 'case') in its real-world context, especially when the boundaries between phenomenon and context may not be clearly evident' (2). Significantly, the salience of the urban context of Dublin in the making of the film called for a method of enquiry which enabled the researcher to focus on a specific event whilst retaining a real-world perspective and simultaneously analysing the contextual conditions in relation to that phenomenon.

Hindi films and non-Indian locations: A mutually beneficial relationship

The use of locations outside India is not uncommon in Hindi films. Since the 1960s, Bollywood films have incorporated sequences shot in faraway locations. A famous example is *Sangam* (Confluence; 1964), which was filmed in Italy, Switzerland and France, establishing a trend for films set in Europe. This tendency has intensified in contemporary films targeting Non-Resident Indians (NRIs) and middle-class South Asians, which often showcase tourist landmarks and transnational lifestyles. At present, it is customary for Hindi films to be set in the UK, America or Australia among other countries. This is usually done to enhance Indian audiences' enjoyment of the film through the display of landscapes remote from their everyday experiences.[1] As Grimaud explains in his ethnography of filmmaking in Bombay: 'the viewer takes pleasure in identifying places, but forgets them as it becomes clear why they were chosen: a bit of exoticism' (227). Exoticisation and 'tourist gaze' are terms that often arise in discussion regarding western representations of other cultures. When elements of Indian culture and landscapes are portrayed in non-Indian film productions, they are likely to raise academic debates that negatively highlight their 'exoticism', which

Figure 1. Actors Salman Khan and Ranvir Shorey on the set of *Ek Tha Tiger* in Dublin's Temple Bar. Source: Photograph: Giovanna Rampazzo.

makes them appealing to Western audiences not familiar with Indian culture. This often applies to films made by South Asian migrant filmmakers resident in Western Europe and North America such as Mira Nair, Deepa Mehta and Gurinder Chadha.[2]

Shohini Chaudhuri, in response to the accusation of exoticism levelled at Deepa Mehta's *Water* (2005), contends that 'exoticisation is a common aesthetic strategy in world cinema and needs to be addressed without the customary moral condemnation' (8). She further argues that these practices are not exclusively employed by Western film industries, as 'catering to a taste for spectacle and exotica has been a long-standing strategy of Indian popular films' (10). In fact, even if aesthetics of exoticism are usually discussed as appealing to Western audiences, Indian popular films have always employed production strategies that in turn allow Indian audiences to see faraway countries as exotic. For according to Chaudhuri:

> While the 'tourist gaze' might be characterised as a particular mode of vision signalling aspiration and access to the privileges of modernity and globalization, it is neither exclusively 'white' nor 'Western' … the so-called 'tourist gaze' is returned in Bollywood sequences in Western metropolises. (10)

The notion of 'tourist gaze' as a socially organised way of seeing typical of contemporary societies, can be linked to Foucauldian theories of surveillance. Notably, Foucault argues that 'the gaze has had great importance among the techniques of power developed in the modern era' (155). John Urry examined the social and cultural implications of the 'tourist gaze', emphasising its plurality and ever-changing nature (173). According to Hollinshead, 'while the tourist gaze approximates to Foucault's institutional gaze of the medic and the professional, it tends to be rather broader in its occurrence and force across society' (9). The power dynamics related to the tourist gaze are arguably fluid rather than fixed and unchangeable. This is motivated by the fact that, 'as patterns of tourism change, so the tourist gaze(s) alter: they are significantly connected to the broader cultural changes of postmodernity' (ibid.).

Significantly, Bollywood sequences set abroad allow Indian audiences to 'return the tourist gaze' to recognisable tourist landmarks that represent dream holiday destinations and suggest the appeal of glossy, consumerist lifestyles. London and Switzerland in *Dilwale Dulhania Le Jayenge* (The Brave Hearted Will Take Away the Bride; 1995), New York in *Kal Ho Naa Ho* (There May or May Not Be a Tomorrow; 2003) and Sydney in *Dil Chahta Hai* (The Heart Desires; 2001) are illustrative examples of the way Western locations are portrayed as desirable holiday destinations for Indian audiences.[3] Jigna Desai argues that these representations are linked to 'the rising dominance of Bollywood and the new urban middle class in India engendered by liberalization' (347), suggesting that wealth and consumerism are not just the privilege of white Western people and neither is the mobilisation of the 'tourist gaze'.

Notably, exploring new locations hitherto not seen in Indian film is a deliberate choice of Bollywood film producers. As Aman Agrawal, a production executive of Yash Raj Films explained in an interview, 'this strategy allows the film to become international and encourages people outside India to get connected to Bollywood'.[4] Significantly, he further pointed out that their films are mainly geared to Indian audiences, so overseas locations are primarily meant to 'appeal to audiences in India who love to see new and unusual places'.[5] The links between travel and cinema have been explored by Amy Corbin in her article *Travelling through Cinema Space* (2014), where she develops the notion of cinema spectatorship as a travel experience. Corbin argues that 'film spectatorship is specifically touristic, and not just a generalized virtual travel experience, because of its entertainment value and its status as an experience you pay for' (316). The following section outlines the links between virtual travel in the form of film spectatorship, allied to the promotion of traditional tourism.

Yash Chopra, founder of Yash Raj Films, is renowned for using Swiss locations characterised by idyllic green valleys and snow-capped mountains, as a backdrop for love scenes in his films. Indian films have a history of setting romantic scenes in mountainous areas and for many years the region of Kashmir, located in the north-west of South Asia, served that purpose. Since the late 1980s, however, Kashmir could no longer be used as a production location due to an ongoing territorial conflict between India and Pakistan. As Qureshi explains, 'Kashmir's scenery and landscape became so popular that lakes, trees and mountains became synonymous with romance in Bollywood'.[6] For this reason, filmmakers resorted to similar landscapes located overseas to effectively convey the romantic feel in their films. Initially, just a few song sequences were set abroad, while the plot was set in India. In the 1990s, however, due to economic liberalisation policies, wealthy Indians living both in and outside the Indian subcontinent started to be seen as potential consumers and investors in the Indian national economy. During those years, Hindi films began setting entire storylines in overseas locations to target growing communities of middle-class South Asians and NRIs. One such example is *Dilwale Dulhania Le Jayenge,* a romantic comedy about two NRIs living in London who meet and fall in love during a rail trip across Europe. The film was also produced by Yash Chopra and filmed in London, Switzerland and India, becoming one of the most successful productions of Hindi cinema. Films such as *Dilwale Dulhania Le Jayenge* boosted tourism to Switzerland to a great extent and Swiss tourism bodies capitalised on the keen interest of Bollywood fans to visit film locations. Switzerland so far has provided locations for over 200 Hindi films, attracting hundreds of thousands of tourists every year. Switzerland does not have historical ties to India nor does it host large Indian communities, suggesting that the vast majority of the Indians visiting the country are tourists attracted by the lush locations appearing in Hindi films.

Over the years it became apparent that Bollywood productions set abroad played an important role in increasing the influx of Indian tourists to the countries featured in the films. By hosting Hindi film productions, governments had the opportunity to use cinema to promote tourism to their countries among wealthy Indian audiences. This notion was reinforced by the constant growth of Indian middle classes since the 1990s. According to Kaur in her essay on representations of the West in Bollywood films: 'economic liberalisation saw the emergence of a globalised Indian middle class. Their conspicuous consumption patterns revealed a highly materialistic and uninhibited urban middle class, constantly fuelled by growing capitalist ambitions' (205).

Irish Government agencies soon became aware of India's rapid economic growth and of the potential of Hindi films to attract Indian tourists to Ireland. The Irish Film Commissioner, Naoise Barry, explained in an interview that since 2004 the Irish Film Board and Tourism Ireland have been trying to build relationships with leading producers of Bollywood films with limited success until *Ek Tha Tiger* was secured.[7] Thus, when Kabir Khan expressed an interest in filming *Ek Tha Tiger* in Dublin, the Irish Government was eager to capitalise on the high profile of the film to promote Ireland as a tourist destination and as a location for more Bollywood films. Since *Ek Tha Tiger* is the first big budget Bollywood production to make extensive use of Dublin locations to date, it is particularly interesting to study the way it was used to promote investments and tourism to Ireland. An important part of the activity of the Irish Film Board is actually to promote Ireland as a location for international film and television productions. This strategy, however, has been criticised as a way to exploit the country for mere financial gain rather than nurturing indigenous Irish filmmaking talent. According to Pettitt, 'Ireland presented and exploited itself as a picturesque location-base (despite the weather) for US and British productions to send over visiting directors and crew enticed by favourable tax relief' (39, 40). Significant tax incentives are in place to attract international film industries and Section 481 of the Irish Taxes Consolidation Act offers up to 28% tax relief on Irish expenditure for international TV and film ventures co-produced with Ireland. As a result, Ireland has a long history of hosting Hollywood and UK productions, providing locations for large-budget productions such as *Saving Private Ryan* (1998), *Braveheart* (1995) and *Far and Away* (1992). Although these films provided employment for Irish crews and brought investment into the economy, in most cases they merely used Irish locations as doubles for other countries. When Hollywood productions have been filmed in Ireland, it has been argued that the locations are commonly reduced to a series of nostalgic and idyllic images, which does not reflect the sociocultural complexities of the country. As Ging contends, 'many of the films produced represent American notions of Irishness rather than articulating the realities of Irish existence, past or present' (190). These problematic representations of Irishness have dominated Irish cinema from its beginnings through well-known international productions such as *The Man of Aran* (1934) and *The Quiet Man* (1952). According to Luke Gibbons, themes such as 'the idealization of the landscape, the persistence of the past, the lure of violence and its ominous association with female sexuality' (117) have characterised Irish cinema since the beginning of 1900. Themes identified by Gibbons have arguably influenced the way the country has been perceived internationally and consequently boosted tourism in some measure.[8] In his seminal work *The Birth of the Clinic*, Foucault introduces the idea of the 'medical gaze', characterised by the dehumanising separation of the patient's body from the patient's identity, as a novel way of producing relevant medical knowledge (109). This concept can arguably be linked with the way the gaze of Irish creative and cultural institutions intentionally promoted superficial and partial notions of Ireland in order to benefit the local tourism industry. The following sections outline how this strategy was employed in the production of *Ek Tha Tiger* to create an appealing imagery aimed at attracting tourists to Ireland (Figure 1).

The relevance of stakeholders in the production of *Ek Tha Tiger*

The Irish Film Commissioner explained that Tourism Ireland[9] worked with the Irish Film Board and Dublin City Council to secure *Ek Tha Tiger* for Ireland, in addition to Trinity College and other agencies to help facilitate filming in the city at reduced costs since the film involved complex and expensive scenes, yet did not have the budget of a Hollywood film. Everybody came on board and waived their fees as they saw the potential of what the film could do in terms of publicity, even if they could not imagine that it would be so successful. The cooperation between the Irish creative, cultural and national institutions who joined forces to facilitate the filming of *Ek Tha Tiger* in Dublin can arguably be described with the aid of stakeholder theory. Freeman's definition of stakeholder is 'any group or individual who can affect or is affected by the achievement of the organization's objectives' (46). The different government agencies and institutions that collaborated in making the production of *Ek Tha Tiger* in Dublin possible can thus be seen as stakeholders in the enterprise of making the film, since they could contribute to the creation of *Ek Tha Tiger* and at the same time benefit from its success. Before hosting *Ek Tha Tiger*, the Irish Film Board and Tourism Ireland had limited success in attracting high-profile Indian film productions to Ireland. As Barry explains:

> It became clear that India was, and continues to be, an important emerging market for Irish tourism ... that film was an important medium by which Indians decide where they are going to go on vacation. So we began working eight years ago with Tourism Ireland office in Mumbai to try to identify the leading producers of Bollywood feature films and we began working to build relationships with those companies. And in the intervening years we had limited success and that success was limited to small elements from bigger movies. It was never the whole movie, only a song and dance sequence ... and the movies those song and dance sequences were in would be smaller movies, not necessarily made by Mumbai based companies, but actually companies based in the south of India, in Chennai. (Interview 13 April 2012)

Having *Ek Tha Tiger* set in Ireland thus represented a big leap forward in the country's attempts to secure Hindi film industry investments, providing a unique opportunity to showcase the beauty of Ireland to a vast number of potential Indian tourists.[10] For this reason, the film became part of an advertising campaign aimed at raising awareness of Ireland as a tourist destination among Indians. Even if India is home to a third of the world's poor,[11] tourism authorities are aware of the presence of affluent Indian audiences with high levels of disposable income, which are also the most sought after clientele for Indian multiplex movie theatres. Athique and Hill analysed the links between the emergence of multiplexes in India and the increasing purchasing power of India's middle classes: 'according to the multiplexes chain, their clientele represents a much more select segment of the middle classes – a segment that can afford to spend above the odds and on non-essentials' (163). Characterised by ticket prices that are 'usually more than triple the rate charged in single-screens theatres'(Ganti 48), multiplexes initially appeared to be mainly vehicles for non-commercial films appealing to educated, middle-class urban audiences. However, multiplexes proved to be instrumental for the domestic success of many recent Hindi blockbusters: '*Bodyguard* (2011), *Agneepath* (Path of Fire; 2012) and *Rowdy Rathore* (2012) have each generated more than one billion rupees at the domestic box office' (Ganti 51). For this reason, a Hindi blockbuster set in Ireland was guaranteed to advertise the country among wealthy audiences who had the financial means to visit the country.

Kabir Khan, the film's director, was instrumental in choosing Dublin as a location for *Ek Tha Tiger*. In an interview, he explained that he needed a unique location, a prestigious college with impressive buildings as a backdrop for the storyline and preferred not to use a British university, since they had appeared many times before in Hindi cinema. Kabir Khan commented: 'when I was writing the script of *Ek Tha Tiger*, I needed a university of repute to set a character in, that's how Trinity College came about'.[12] The director had been to Trinity College in 1995 to interview then President Mary Robinson and was impressed by the architecture of the place, so he decided to use it as a location for the film. As Barry recalls: 'it was very good luck on our part in that the first third of the movie takes place in a university ... in this case Kabir knew about Trinity College Dublin, so he called me and asked if we could host a visit for him and his creative team'.[13] However, the decision to use Dublin as a location was motivated by the script and by the director's choice rather than by effective advertising campaigns or incentives offered by government agencies. As Avtar Panesar, Vice President of International Operations at Yash Raj Films, confirmed in an interview: 'everything is really driven by the script and what the director wants to do with it; so it's never the case that we always want to shoot at a particular place; if it fits the script, if it works, we then make use of the country as a location'.[14]

When Yash Raj Films contacted Trinity College enquiring about the possibility to film *Ek Tha Tiger* on campus, the university had been closed to film crews for almost 20 years. However, Vice-Provost Michael Marsh agreed to the filming of *Ek Tha Tiger*, seeing the potential of this project as an advertising tool for the university. In fact, the filming of *Ek Tha Tiger* was included in a Trinity College promotional video and delegations from Trinity College went to India upon the film's release to conduct a promotional campaign aimed at attracting prospective Indian students. Details on how the film was used as a promotional tool for Trinity College are addressed later in this article.

Advertising Ireland through Bollywood: *Ek Tha Tiger* as a promotional vehicle

The Irish Government worked closely with Yash Raj Films who supported Ireland's advertising campaign as part of their production agreement to shoot the film in Ireland (Figure 2). As Panesar noted 'we came up with many promos which highlighted Ireland as part of the campaign here, and the Irish Tourism Board actually played these promos out here in India, because that's the market they wanted to target'.[15] Yash Raj Films agreed to the film being used to promote Ireland in order to benefit from reduced fees for filming on location. These dynamics remind us that the production of the film depended on establishing a mutually advantageous relationship between Yash Raj Films and Irish tourism agencies, making sure

Figure 2. Advertisement linked to *Ek Tha Tiger* on Tourism Ireland website upon the film's release. Source: Image: www.TourismIreland.com.

that the needs of the latter were effectively met. This is in line with tenets of stakeholder theory, since 'a fundamental thesis of stakeholder-based arguments is that organizations should be managed in the interest of all their constituents, not only in the interest of shareholders' (Laplume et al. 1153). Barry stated in an interview that the production benefited from tax incentives, complimentary visas and reduced location fees, but did not receive any direct funding from Ireland.[16]

The collaboration between Tourism Ireland and Yash Raj Films in the creation of imagery designed to cultivate curiosity among Indian viewers by portraying Ireland in an alluring way, suggests that the construction and development of people's gaze as tourists depends on specific marketing and communication strategies. To this end, Urry and Larsen argue that 'the concept of the gaze highlights that looking is a learned ability and that the pure and innocent eye is a myth' (Urry and Larsen 1). Urry discusses how people are encouraged to look at new environments using a tourist gaze similar to Foucault's 'medical gaze' (1). According to Urry, the tourist gaze is also professionally crafted and controlled: 'this gaze is as socially organised and systematised as is the gaze of the medic' (Ibid.). The images of Ireland associated with *Ek Tha Tiger* mobilise a superficial view of the city as charming, colourful and cosmopolitan, encouraging the viewer/tourist to focus on these aspects of the place rather than delving into the complexities of Irish history and society. These images were subsequently circulated across the internet by Tourism Ireland upon the film's release to advertise the country. A few days before the release of the film, Tourism Ireland Chief, Niall Gibbons stated that:

> There is tremendous excitement in India, and among the Indian Diaspora, about this week's release of *Ek Tha Tiger* and we are confident that it will help increase awareness of the island of Ireland among Indian travellers who are always on the look-out for new destinations to explore.[17]

Irish Tourism authorities are aware that carefully crafted images of Ireland can potentially lure tourists to visit the country. To this end, the imagery of Ireland promoted by *Ek Tha*

Tiger points to the power of institutions that influence what the viewer should see and know about a country. Urry and Larsen examine these dynamics using Foucauldian notions of surveillance and power relations: 'following Foucault, we can see this making of seductive images and destinations as an institutional mediation by 'expert gazes' within which spectacle and surveillance intersect and power-knowledge relations are played out' (Urry and Larsen 173). The way Dublin is framed in *Ek Tha Tiger* reveals how the 'expert gaze' of filmmakers can be complicit in constructing a tourist gaze for audiences. In fact, overt advertisement for Dublin was discernible across action sequences set in Dublin city centre, showcasing Dublin's most touristic areas including the Luas train.[18]

In one chase sequence, the protagonist follows a Pakistani secret agent across the Temple Bar[19] area; a close up of the sign of the Temple Bar Trading Company™ helps locate this scene within the city, suggesting the importance of the location, even if this shot has no real relevance in the narrative of the film. This was clearly a way to highlight the shopping opportunities offered by the area and to justify the disruption to businesses caused by the film sets. 'Dublin shop owners in general had a positive attitude towards the filming and were happy to come on board as they saw the potential of what the film could do', explained Dermot Cleary, the film's Location Manager.[20] A run down area at risk of demolition until the 1980s, Temple Bar is now one of Dublin's main tourist attractions and is widely advertised as 'Dublin's cultural and entertainment quarter' and as a site of cultural and historical significance. Temple Bar, however, is what Maeve Connolly defines as 'a large scale example of staged-authenticity' (2). Notably, the colourful shop fronts and impressive facades that characterise the area are actually visible material remnants of the sets of a big budget Hollywood production, *Far and Away* (1992). Thus, film sets belonging to an American filmic representation of Ireland are actually advertised as authentic and quintessentially Irish. Connolly explains that even if the film 'was received as highly 'unauthentic', the sets were retained by popular demand and became part of the scenery of Temple Bar' (2). This can be linked to an attempt of the locals to control and direct the tourist gaze in order to prevent tourists from knowing aspects of Irish life and society perceived as irrelevant to outsiders: 'apparently authentic back-stages may be artificially created by local people and entrepreneurs to redirect the gaze and hence reduce the degree of intrusion' (Crawshaw and Urry 178). These notions recall Foucauldian theories surrounding the interrelation of power and knowledge and the pervasive nature of power, which is not prerogative of few repressive institutions, but rather it is omnipresent and in constant flux. According to Foucault, power 'induces pleasures, forms knowledge, produces discourse. It needs to be considered as a productive network which runs through the whole social body' (119).

The exteriors and interiors of traditional pubs are shown during the film's chase sequence; here signs advertising Guinness beer and a medium shot of a gentleman sipping a pint of the same beverage suggest that drinking alcohol is a distinctive element of Irish social life and culture. Across Temple Bar, the constant advertisement of beer and spirits encourages tourists to consume these beverages to participate in an authentic experience of Irishness. These representations, however, are not unproblematic given that they are linked to negative Irish stereotypes widespread in England. Stereotypes are overgeneralisations of the characteristics of a cultural or social group and 'negative stereotyping is seen as a method of reiterating a binaristic contrast as a negative group difference' (Bowe et al. 8). Notably, Mary J. Hickman in her analysis of the experience of Irish migrants in Britain during the twentieth century contends that 'English people continued to associate the Irish with drink, fighting and dirt' (298). Moreover, 'drunkenness has provided one of the core stereotypes of Irishness; its addiction being linked to the supposed frail control which Irish people have over their bodies' (Nagle 118). Therefore, it can be argued that the touristic promotion of Ireland is organised around derogatory representations of Irish culture.

Determined to exploit the film to advertise Ireland among South Asian communities in and outside India, Tourism Ireland teamed up with Yash Raj Films and Ethiad airlines, organising an extensive advertising campaign aimed at audiences in India and in the Gulf countries. They used dinner events upon the release of the film, television and digital advertising and organised competitions through social media such as Facebook and online booking platforms such as Yatra.com. Some six days following the launch of the film on 15 August 2012, Tourism Ireland's Indian Facebook page had gained over 23,000 fans, up from 10,000 before the release[21]; and over one year later the page had about 90,000 fans. In the months following the release of *Ek Tha Tiger* in 2012, the Irish Central Statistics Office recorded an increase in tourism from long-haul destinations – visits to the Tourism Ireland website further increased since the release of the film.[22] Irish tourism authorities, however, were determined to continue targeting Indian tourists and to further capitalise on the success of the finished film. For example, in January 2014 Tourism Ireland organised their first-ever India seminar aimed at Irish tourism enterprises interested in welcoming Indian tourists. During the seminar Irish agencies declared their aim of increasing the numbers of Indian tourists visiting Ireland. Minister for Transport, Tourism and Sport, Leo Varadkar,[23] commented: 'India is one of the fastest-growing tourism markets in the world. Although the numbers visiting Ireland are relatively small, the Indian market has significant potential for growth'.[24] Tourism Ireland confirmed their intention to continue their collaboration with the Irish Film Board and Northern Ireland Screen, targeting top Bollywood producers and highlighting the locations available around the island of Ireland.[25] Even if no other major Hindi production has to date made use of locations in the Republic of Ireland since *Ek Tha Tiger*,[26] the film definitely established a foundation for future collaboration between Indian entertainment industries and Irish creative and cultural industries.

Promoting Trinity College Dublin in India

Trinity College was founded in 1592 by Queen Elizabeth I and chosen as a location for the film, especially for its monumental historic buildings. The university has long-standing links to South Asia, first established with the inauguration of the chair of Oriental Languages in 1762. It has been regularly hosting international students from India since the nineteenth century, and in 2009, the Trinity College South Asia initiative was launched to strengthen the university's relationship with India. The prominent role of Trinity College in *Ek Tha Tiger*'s storyline was crucially part of a promotional campaign already in place at Trinity College and linked to government agencies eager to attract Indian students. As Olivia Waters of the Trinity College Global Relations Office noted:

> India has taken on a new level, not just here in Trinity but in Ireland: Education in Ireland, the brand that is run by Enterprise Ireland, see India as a huge marketplace for Ireland. Activity has really ramped up in this area. So we have been working in India but *Ek Tha Tiger* gave us a platform to improve our visibility and raise our profile around the country. (Interview 4 October 2012)

Figure 3. Still from *Ek Tha Tiger* – The dance sequence at Trinity College.

For this reason, the university's office for Global Relations arranged for the making of a promotional video for Trinity College[27] including interviews with South Asian students, lecturers, crew members, featuring scenes of the filming of *Ek Tha Tiger* around campus and highlighting the way students had the opportunity to interact with the film's production. Several other internationally renowned films have included scenes shot around campus: for example, the Jedi Library in *Star Wars Episode II* (2002) is the Long Room, the main chamber of the Trinity College Old Library; *Educating Rita* (1983) was filmed in Trinity College; in *Michael Collins* (1996) the Dail debate was filmed in the 1937 Reading Room. As Trinity College's Vice-Provost for Global Relations, Jane Olhmeyer, explained in an interview: 'we always use a film as a point of reference for prospective students'.[28] However, *Ek Tha Tiger* was the first film with an overt Trinity College storyline, so it had the potential to be more effective in granting visibility to the university (Figure 3). Upon the release of the film, delegations from Trinity College went to India to conduct a promotional campaign aimed at attracting prospective students; special screenings of *Ek Tha Tiger* were hosted in five Indian cities Mumbai, Bangalore, Chennai, Calcutta and Delhi. Information on the filming of *Ek Tha Tiger* was also included on the university's website.[29] As Ohlmeyer recalls: 'we worked very closely with Yash Raj Films. They said, 'we will give you access to clips for student recruitment purposes' and then we came up with this idea of actually holding screenings across India'.[30] In August 2012, Yash Chopra, founder of Yash Raj Films, also received a Trinity College honorary professorship for his significant contribution to Indian cinema.[31] A special screening of *Ek Tha Tiger* was held at Trinity College in September 2012; on that occasion Kabir Khan also gave a master class to several Trinity College film and drama students.[32] The filming of *Ek Tha Tiger* proved to be beneficial in raising the profile of the university; as Waters confirmed: 'we have seen an increase in activity on the website from India, an increase in applications for our postgraduate scholarships, an increase in interest from schools that we would have had relationships with'.[33]

The reception of *Ek Tha Tiger*: Dublin and worldwide

The film opened worldwide on 15 August 2012 and its Dublin premiere at the Irish Film Institute marked the launch of the first Mela festival of Dublin.[34] This event was used by Yash Raj Films to promote the film among Irish-based audiences. According to Panesar, 'upon the release of *Ek Tha Tiger*, on 15 August, we used the event to drive the campaign, and we worked closely with the cinema, as well as the Mela to try and garner as much attention as we possibly could'.[35] On the other hand, collaborating with Yash Raj Films and hosting the premiere of a film which promised to be an international success was also advantageous for the Irish Film Institute and for the Indian cultural organisation behind the Mela in terms of raising their public profile and improving awareness about their activities. This mutually beneficial collaboration between an internationally renowned film production company and local Irish cultural associations confirms the validity of Freeman's stakeholder management principles as he cautioned managers to 'take into account all of those groups and individuals that can affect, or are affected by, the accomplishment of the business enterprise' (25). Notably, tickets to the *Ek That Tiger* premiere were sold out and it unfolded as a high-profile event introduced by then Minister for Culture Jimmy Deenihan and Film Commissioner Naoise Barry.

Ek Tha Tiger was screened at Cineworld Dublin[36] between 15 August and 3 September 2012 and was well received by audiences. Several viewers were disappointed by its storyline comparing it with Kabir Khan's previous features – the thought-provoking political dramas *Kabul Express* (2006) and *New York* (2009). However, they enjoyed the film's song and action sequences, especially the one involving the Luas, and liked the way Dublin was portrayed in it. A Bollywood fan commented, 'I was disappointed by the story: I was expecting something like *New York* … But I love the tram scene in Dublin! And I love the song where they dance in Trinity College'. 'I really enjoyed the film', said Bharath Kumar, founder of Unitas Isac and organiser of the Mela festival. Members of the film's crew also appreciated the finished film: 'the film was really good, well directed and Dublin looks really good in it', said Dermot Cleary, the film's Location Manager. Olivia Waters was also pleasantly surprised: 'I loved the film! I was surprised by the humour in it, I didn't think it followed the usual Bollywood format … I thought Dublin came across as a fun, young city'. The makers of the *Ek Tha Tiger* wanted the locales portrayed in the film to be part of the spectacle expected from a blockbuster and they were clearly successful in their intent to show Dublin as a vibrant and exciting city. This upbeat and modern representation is in line with a new image of Ireland promoted since the 1990s, when the economic boom prompted the media to refashion an appealing portrayal of the country, which denied its problematic past and social struggles in order to raise its international appeal. 'The reinvented Ireland of the Celtic Tiger is based on the creation of a 'modern, liberal, progressive, multicultural' image fashioned according to the need for international acceptance' (Kirby et al. 197). Irish films of the late 1990s and early 2000s moved away from the gritty social realism that characterised productions of the 1970s and 1980s, aiming instead to portray Ireland as liberal, urban and successful. Films such as *About Adam* (1999) and *When Brendan Met Trudy* (2001) focus on young and lively urbanites, highlighting the newfound cosmopolitanism and multiculturalism of Dublin, deliberately ignoring any of the social problems that afflict contemporary Ireland such as crime, alcoholism, poverty, homelessness and drug abuse. As Ging contends, 'our national cinema is moving steadily toward easy, globally digestible narratives' (185). *Waking Ned* (1999) and *The Closer You Get* (2000) present an idyllic view of rural Ireland aimed at the American market. According to Ging, these films deny 'that Ireland is a complex and changing nation with a troubled sense of self-identity, pandering instead to a largely mainstream American understanding of Irishness' (187). In a similar way, it can be argued that *Ek Tha Tiger* carefully avoided representing any kind of complexity or social issues present in the underbelly of the charming and cosmopolitan Irish capital, constructing instead a simplistic image of Ireland that requires a minimum of cross-cultural understanding or critical engagement on the part of the viewer. This kind of representation is in line with long-standing strategies supported by government agencies to promote the country internationally and create a marketable version of Irishness. Representing Ireland through stereotypes, however, is problematic since it promotes unrealistic cognitive associations and expectations about Irish society by presenting limited and partial notions of the country and its culture. To this end, Bowe et al. argue that 'stereotypes, whether positive or negative, limit our understanding of human behaviour and can lead to miscommunications in intercultural discourse' (10).

Although questionable, the cultural representations showcased in *Ek Tha Tiger* were extremely well received by audiences, as the film has been hugely successful breaking several box office records in India and achieving worldwide gross of 3.25 billion Rupees (39 million Euro).[37] It became the second highest grossing Bollywood film of all time, surpassed only by *3 Idiots* (2009). The film's box office success was later exceeded by blockbusters such as *Chennai Express* (2013) and *Dhoom 3* (Blast 3; 2013).[38] Kabir Khan's third feature film received positive to mixed reviews from Indian critics. Taran Adarsh of *Bollywood Hungama* rated the film 4.5 stars out of 5, calling it a 'high octane thriller that works big time. This one has style and substance, both, besides dazzling action, stunning international locales and stylish execution'.[39] Anupama Chopra of *Hindustan Times* gave it 3 stars out of 5 and said that the film was Salman Khan's best since *Dabangg*; it had more story coherence and emotions than Khan's recent films.[40] In the Irish press, the film was praised mainly for its potential to attract tourists to Ireland [41] confirming the notion that the most significant Irish–Indian coproduction to date was considered mainly a vehicle for Irish national promotion.

This discussion has endeavoured to demonstrate how both the underlying production concerns of *Ek Tha Tiger* and audience participation and engagement with the film are intricately imbricated in Dublin's urban life – a deliberately chosen context for the film characterised by the nationally iconic appearance of established and stereotyped markers of 'Ireland' and 'Irishness'. By way of narrating the arc of the film's production, this article has outlined how Irish Government agencies and Bollywood collaborated in the making of a blockbuster, ostensibly used as an advertising tool to attract Indian tourists, students and investments to Ireland. This discussion further indicates how *Ek Tha Tiger* produced a 'tourist gaze' for audiences, shaping their perception of Dublin and Irish culture according to institutionally choreographed images of charm and cosmopolitanism. In so doing, the film plays on existing clichés and stereotypes surrounding Irish culture and identity, showcasing postcard-like views of Dublin thus far featured in commercial Irish films and international productions set in Ireland. These representations of Irishness were well received by audiences both in Ireland and abroad and proved to be effective in boosting tourism to Ireland. The production of *Ek Tha Tiger* in Dublin thus confirmed the effectiveness of Bollywood cinema in constructing spectacular and appealing, albeit partial and potentially misleading, notions of Irish urban life.

Research interests

Globalisation of Indian cinema; transnational reception of popular Hindi films; ethnography of Hindi film audiences; Indian film festivals and cinephilia; practices of Hindi films exhibition and consumption in the Irish context; Irish Indian co-productions and diasporic films.

Notes

1. Narratives displaced from the Indian national context can also enable the representations of liminal fantasies in a non-threatening manner, suggesting that morally questionable behaviours can happen in other places but not in India.
2. As Adrian Athique explains, the works of these directors of Indian origin 'have frequently been conflated with Bollywood in the Western media. Both Indian and expatriate directors have benefited from this fallacy: mainstream Indian films have been associated, for example, with the success of Nair's *Monsoon Wedding* (2001), whilst the 'colour as culture' connotations of Bollywood branding have been used to market the films of non-resident Indian (or NRI) directors, such as Chadha's *Bride and Prejudice* (2004)' (Athique 301).
3. These films showcasing the life of NRIs arguably serve the function of discouraging diasporic groups from adopting Western moral standards through the display of themes promoting traditional Indian values. This strategy is in line with middle-class ideologies focused on preserving morality and tradition against Western influences. As Kaur contends, these themes are 'specifically family values, moral superiority, true (unpolluted) love, the sacrifice of individual desires for greater good of the family/community, and the struggle and victory of the Indian Diaspora in preserving their cultural universe through Indian rites of passages in an alien environment (Kaur 200, 201).'
4. Agrawal, Aman. Yash Raj Films Production Executive. Interview 15 Oct. 2011.
5. Ibid.
6. Qureshi, Irna. 'Bollywood in Britain – The Legacy of Yash Chopra'. 23 Oct. 2012. Theguardian.com. Web. 15 Nov. 2013. <http://www.theguardian.com/uk/the-northerner/2012/oct/23/lakedistrict-scotland-northern-ireland-extra>.
7. Barry, Naoise. Irish Film Commissioner. Interview 13 Apr. 2012.
8. 'The Quiet Man' – The Movie That Put Ireland on the Tourist Map – *Film Ireland* – 1 Nov. 2011. Web. 20 May 2014. <http://filmireland.net/2011/11/01/the-quiet-man-the-movie-that-put-ireland-on-the-tourist-map/>.
9. A government agency in charge of the promotion of Ireland as a tourist destination. Web. 10 Dec. 2011. <https://www.tourismireland.com/>.
10. For more on Irish film locations used to promote tourism see O'Connor and Bolan (1–12).
11. Mashru, Ram. 'India's Growing Urban Poverty Crisis'. *The Diplomat* 4 Mar. 2014. Web. 25 May 2014. <http://thediplomat.com/2014/03/indias-growing-urban-poverty-crisis/>.
12. Giovanna, Maria. 'Chalo Ireland: Will Ek Tha Tiger Be Dublin's Lucky Charm?' 1 Sep. 2012. Firstpost.com. Web. 15 Sept. 2012. <http://www.firstpost.com/world/chalo-ireland-will-ek-tha-tiger-be-dublins-lucky-charm-436928.html>.
13. Barry, Naoise. Irish Film Commissioner. Interview 13 Apr. 2012.
14. Panesar, Avtar. Vice President of International Operations at Yash Raj Films. Interview 28 Feb. 2013.
15. Ibid.
16. Barry, Naoise. Irish Film Commissioner. Interview 13 Apr. 2012.
17. Bollywood film shot in Dublin expected to be watched by 100 million people. Web. 15 Sept. 2012. <http://www.thejournal.ie/bollywood-film-shot-in-dublin-expected-to-be-watched-by-100-million-people-557882-Aug2012/>.
18. Luas means 'speed' in Irish and is a tram (or light rail system) serving Dublin.
19. Temple Bar is a designated cultural quarter in Dublin situated on the south bank of the river Liffey. It is known for its lively nightlife and its popularity among tourists.

20. Cleary, Dermot. Location Manager. Interview 3 Sep. 2012.
21. Munshi, Neil. 'The Irish Look for the Luck of the Indians … in Bollywood'. 21 Aug. 2012. Web. 30 Aug. 2012. <http://blogs.ft.com/beyond-brics/2012/08/21/the-irish-look-for-the-luck-of-the-indians-in-bollywood/#axzz24BxzquWN>.
22. Tourism Ireland Comment on CSO Figures for December 2012–February 2013. Web. 10 Apr. 2013. <http://www.tourismireland.com/Home!/About-Us/Press-Releases/2013/Tourism-Ireland-Comment-on-CSO-Figures-for-Decembe.aspx>.
23. Leo Varadkar is the son of an Indian doctor from Mumbai and an Irish nurse (who met while working together in a hospital in Slough, England). His political career has been marked by controversy, an example being his proposal of a voluntary repatriation scheme for unemployed migrants, which attracted accusations of racism. Ghosh, Palash. 'Leo Varadkar: Could This Indian Man One Day Become Prime Minister Of Ireland?' 24 Jul. 2013. Web. 20 May 2014. <http://www.ibtimes.com/leo-varadkar-could-indian-man-one-day-become-prime-minister-ireland-1359033>.
24. Targeting Indian Tourists for the Island of Ireland. Web. 15 Feb. 2014. <https://www.tourismireland.com/Home!/About-Us/Press-Releases/2014/Targeting-Indian-Tourists-for-the-Island-of-Irelan.aspx>.
25. Ibid.
26. The Hindi production *Teraa Surroor* (Your Passion; Shawn Arranha, 2016) featuring Bollywood actor and music composer Himesh Reshammiya, was filmed in Dublin in September 2015. *Teraa Surroor* had a much smaller budget compared to *Ek Tha Tiger* and it did not include spectacular dance sequences or major Bollywood stars. For such reasons it did not attract as much attention from the media or from fans and was not actively used to promote Ireland as a tourist destination.
27. Bollywood Comes to Trinity College Dublin – Filming of Ek Tha Tiger at TCD. Web. 15 Sept. 2012. <https://www.youtube.com/watch?v=fpE2-AOAIEU>.
28. Ohlmeyer, Jane. Trinity College Vice Provost for Global Relations. Interview 15 Oct. 2012.
29. Bollywood Film Shot on Location at Trinity College Dublin Launches in India and Dublin. Web. 15 Sept. 2013. <https://www.tcd.ie/globalrelations/news/Ek%20Tha%20Tiger%20launch.php>.
30. Ohlmeyer, Jane. Interview 15 Oct. 2012.
31. Bollywood's Most Influential Filmmaker, Yash Chopra, Receives Honorary Professorship from Trinity College Dublin, Marking 100 Years of Bollywood Film. Web. 15 Sept. 2012. <https://www.tcd.ie/Communications/news/pressreleases/pressRelease.php?headerID=2652&pressReleaseArchive=2012>.
32. Yash Chopra was also supposed to give a master class at Trinity College later in 2012, but he sadly passed away on 21 October 2012.
33. Waters, Olivia. Trinity College Communications and Global Relations Office. Interview 4 Oct. 2012.
34. Mela means large gathering in Sanskrit and Mela festivals are South Asian cultural fairs organised in various countries hosting Indian communities such as the UK, but they had never been organised in Ireland before August 2012. Dublin Mela was organised by Unitas Isac, a not for profit organisation set up by members of the Indian Diaspora in Ireland with the aim of promoting community integration through sport, arts and culture. The festival took place between 15 and 19 August, including events such as an art exhibition, Indian dance and sports workshops and a day-long family event centred on performances of South Asian dance and music.
35. Panesar, Avtar. Vice-President of International Operations at Yash Raj Films. Interview 28 Feb. 2013.
36. Cineworld Dublin is a 17-screen multiplex located in Dublin city centre. Since 2006 Cineworld Dublin has been the only cinema in the Irish capital which regularly screens popular Indian films.
37. Chennai Express Crosses *Ek Tha Tiger* Worldwide In Ten Days. Web. 30 Aug. 2013. <http://www.boxofficeindia.com/boxnewsdetail.php?page=shownews&articleid=5979&nCat=>.

38. At the time of writing the highest grossing Bollywood film ever is PK (Rajkumar Hirani, 2014).
39. Adarsh, Taran. 'Ek Tha Tiger'. 15 Aug. 2012. Web. 30 Aug. 2012. <http://www.bollywoodhungama.com/moviemicro/criticreview/id/545809>.
40. Chopra, Anupama. 'Anupama Chopra's Review: Ek Tha Tiger'. 16 Aug. 2012. Web. 30 Aug. 2012. <http://www.hindustantimes.com/Entertainment/Reviews/Anupama-Chopra-s-review-Ek-Tha-Tiger/Article1-914239.aspx#sthash.IPEZpvVK.dpuf>.
41. Rupee Tuesday – 21 Aug. 2012. Web. 30 Aug. 2012. <http://www.broadsheet.ie/2012/08/21/rupee-tuesday/>.

Acknowledgements

I wish to acknowledge my supervisors and colleagues at the Centre for Transcultural Research and Media Practice, Dublin Institute of Technology, for their ongoing support and guidance. I am grateful to the peer reviewers whose comments helped improve and clarify this article.

Disclosure statement

No potential conflict of interest was reported by the author.

ORCID

Giovanna Rampazzo http://orcid.org/0000-0001-8653-991X

References

Athique A. "The 'Crossover' Audience: Mediated Multiculturalism and the Indian Film." *Continuum: Journal of Media & Cultural Studies* 22.3 (2008): 299–311.
Athique A., and D. Hill. *The Multiplex in India: A Cultural Economy of Urban Leisure*. London: Routledge, 2010.
Bowe H., K. Martin, and H. Manns. *Communication Across Cultures: Mutual Understanding in a Global World*. 2nd ed. Cambridge: Cambridge University Press, 2014.
Chaudhuri S. "Snake Charmers and Child Brides: Deepa Mehta's Water, 'Exotic' Representation, and the Cross-cultural Spectatorship of South Asian migrant Cinema." *South Asian Popular Culture* 7.1 (2009): 7–20.
Connolly M. "Postcard from Dublin." *SuperUmbau* (Interdisciplinary Urban Project Newspaper), Winter Edition, 1998.
Corbin A. "Travelling through Cinema Space: The Film Spectator as Tourist." *Continuum: Journal of Media and Cultural Studies* 28.3 (2014): 314–29.
Crawshaw C., and J. Urry. "Tourism and the Photographic Eye." *Touring Cultures: Transformations in Travel and Theory*. Ed. C. Rojek and J. Urry. London: Routledge, 1997. 176–95.

Creswell J.W. *Research Design: Qualitative, Quantitative and Mixed Approaches*. London: Sage, 2014.
Desai, J. "Bollywood, USA Diasporas Nations and the State of Cinema." *Transnational South Asians: the Making of a Neo Diaspora*. Eds. S. Koshy and R. Radhakrishnan. Oxford: Oxford University Press, 2008. 345–364.
Freeman R.E. *Strategic Management: A Stakeholder Approach*. Boston, MA: Pitman, 1984.
Foucault M. *The Birth of the Clinic*. London: Travistock, 1976.
Foucault M. "Truth and Power." *Power/Knowledge: Selected Interviews and Other Writings, 1972–77*. Ed. C Gordon. New York, NY: Pantheon Books, 1980. 109–45.
Foucault M. "The Eye of Power." *Power/Knowledge: Selected Interviews and Other Writings, 1972–77*. Ed. C Gordon. New York, NY: Pantheon Books, 1980. 146–65.
Ganti T. *Producing Bollywood: Inside the Contemporary Hindi Film Industry*. Durham, NC: Duke University Press, 2012.
Ganti T. *Bollywood: A Guidebook to Popular Hindi Cinema*. 2nd ed. London: Routledge, 2013.
Gibbons, L. *Transformations in Irish Culture*. Cork: Cork University Press, 1996.
Ging D. "Screening the Green: Cinema under the Celtic Tiger." *Reinventing Ireland: Culture and the Celtic Tiger*. Ed. P Kirby, L Gibbons and M Cronin. London: Pluto Press, 2002. 177–195.
Grimaud E. *Bollywood Film Studio, ou, Comment les Films se Font à Bombay*. Paris: CNRS Editions, 2003.
Hickman MJ. "Reconstructing Deconstructing 'Race': British Political Discourses about the Irish in Britain." *Ethnic and Racial Studies* 21.2 (1998): 288–307.
Hollinshead K. "Surveillance of the Worlds of Tourism: Foucault and the Eye-of-power." *Tourism Management* 20.1 (1999): 7–23.
Kaur R. "Viewing the West through Bollywood: A Celluliod Occident in the Making." *Contemporary South Asia* 11.2 (2002): 199–209.
Kirby P., L. Gibbons, and M. Cronin, eds. *Reinventing Ireland*. London: Pluto Press, 2002.
Laplume A.O., K. Sonpar, and R.A. Litz. "Stakeholder Theory: Reviewing a Theory That Moves Us." *Journal of Management* 34.6 (December 2008): 1152–89.
Nagle J. *Multiculturalism's Double-bind: Creating Inclusivity, Cosmopolitanism and Difference*. Farnham: Ashgate Publishing Ltd., 2009.
O'Connor N., and P. Bolan. "Creating a Sustainable Brand for Northern Ireland Through Film Induced Tourism." *Tourism, Culture & Communication* 8 (2008): 1–12.
Pettitt L. *Screening Ireland: Film and Television Representation*. Manchester; New York: Manchester University Press, 2000.
Urry J. *The Tourist Gaze: Leisure and Travel in Contemporary Societies*. London: Sage, 1990.
Urry J. "The Tourist Gaze 'Revisited.'" *American Behavioral Scientist* 36.2 (1992): 172–86.
Urry, J., and J. Larsen. *The Tourist Gaze 3.0*. London: Sage, 2012.
Yin R.K. *Case Study Research: Design and Methods*. 5th ed. London: Sage, 2014.

Filmography

About Adam. Dir. Gerard Stembridge, 1999.
Agneepath (Path of Fire). Dir. Karan Malhotra, 2012.
Bodyguard. Dir. Siddique, 2011.
Braveheart. Dir. Mel Gibson, 1995.
Chennai Express. Dir. Rohit Shetty, 2013.
Dabangg (Fearless). Dir. Abhinav Kashyap, 2010.
Dabangg 2 (Fearless 2). Dir. Arbaaz Khan, 2012.
Dil Chahta Hai (The Heart Desires). Dir. Farhan Akhtar, 2001.
Dilwale Dulhania Le Jayenge (The Brave Hearted Will Take Away the Bride). Dir. Aditya Chopra, 1995.
Dhoom 3 (Blast 3). Dir. Vijay Krishna Acharya, 2013.
Educating Rita. Dir. Lewis Gilbert, 1983.
Ek Tha Tiger. Dir. Kabir Khan, 2012.
Far and Away. Dir. Ron Howard, 1992.

Kabul Express. Dir. Kabir Khan, 2006.
Kal Ho Naa Ho (There May or May Not Be a Tomorrow). Dirs. Nikhil Advani, Ron Reid Jr., 2003.
Michael Collins. Dir. Neil Jordan, 1996.
New York. Dir. Kabir Khan, 2009.
Rowdy Rathore. Dir. Prabhu Deva, 2012.
Sangam (Confluence). Dir. Raj Kapoor, 1964.
Saving Private Ryan. Dir. Steven Spielberg, 1998.
Star Wars Episode II. Dir. George Lucas, 2002.
Teraa Surroor (Your Passion). Dir. Shawn Arranha, 2016.
The Closer You Get. Dir. Aileen Ritchie, 2000.
The Man of Aran. Dir. Robert J. Flaherty, 1934.
The Quiet Man. Dir. John Ford, 1952.
Three Idiots. Dir. Rajkumar Irani, 2009.
Waking Ned. Dir. Kirk Jones, 1999.
When Brendan Met Trudy. Dir. Kieron J. Walsh, 2001.
Zindagi Na Milegi Dobara (You Don't Live Twice). Dir. Zoya Akhtar, 2011.

'New Bollywood' and the emergence of a 'Production House' culture

Amrita Goswami

ABSTRACT
This article focuses on the current phase in the Hindi Film Industry in Bombay which is characterized by a new corporate logic coming into play since 2000 that looks at a film as a product, and then goes about packaging it, branding it and presenting it to a predetermined audience. This shift is characteristic of the processes of the mainstream film industry with the onset of corporate-run Production Houses (It is a conscious decision on my part to use the term 'Production House' and not Studios.) that came about with the transition of the Hindi film industry from an unorganized industry to that of a corporatized body after being accorded Industry status in 1998 ('Film Accorded Industry Status', *Business Line*, October 19, 2000 http://www.indiaserver.com/businessline/2000/10/19/stories/141918re.htm). I am using the term 'Production House/s' despite the fact that film companies use the term *Studio* in their nomenclature, because unlike the Studios in the early Indian cinema landscape, these are multinational corporations that have an entirely different logic of film production and labour. This logic is what I attempt to discuss in this article. The methodology I have used for arriving at my understanding of how this Production House culture works is informed by ethnographic techniques of qualitative interviews with people working in the Hindi Film Industry in different capacities, participant observation on locations and sets, and using the technique of observing a day-in-the-life of an industry professional at work.

The 'New Bollywood' moment

To understand the functioning of Production Houses, it is important to understand that moment in the Hindi Film Industry which paved the way for a Corporate led approach towards film production, distribution and circulation.

In this article, I have located my arguments within the area of Film Industry studies. Since Hollywood forms the best analogy for mainstream cinemas in India, I have looked at the work on the Hollywood industry, the best known of which is by Bordwell, Staiger and Thompson (xvi–xvii) who describe classical Hollywood cinema as 'a distinct artistic and economic phenomenon' (xvi–xvii) and have attempted to show how 'the concept of a mode of film practice can historicize textual analysis and connect the history of film style to the history of the motion picture industry' (xvii). Here, I would like to draw the reader's attention to the commodity nature of Hindi films by exploring the process that is involved in turning various raw materials[1] and labour into feature films that are distributed, advertised and exhibited as commodities to audiences. In this context, Bordwell's recent work on the contemporary Hollywood Industry where he analyses 'New Hollywood' as a corporate body that functions increasingly through business strategies with respect to star competition, special effects, film franchises consisting of sequels, the promotional ventures and tie-ups with companies and global markets and a tightly marked timeline for the release of films (1) is very useful for me. Furthermore, McDonald and Wasko (25–26) point out that Hollywood has reorganized itself in contemporary times as the 'dominant global entertainment machine' characteristics of which include 'conglomeration, diversification, transnationalisation of ownership, multiplication of distribution outlets, escalating production budgets, film event production, exploitation of ancillary markets, the freelance market for creative and craft labour, and the global dispersal of production' (4). Analysing the practice of branding, the usage of corporate logos and the industrial politics surrounding the development of branded texts, properties and spaces, Paul Grainge considers the relation of branding to the emergent principle of 'total entertainment' (55–59). Drawing inspiration from these works, I draw parallels with the Hindi film industry by marking a similar moment of transformation in the business of film-making leading to newer production structures, branding and marketing of films and disaggregation of products and audiences, for which I find the term 'New Bollywood' very appropriate. Gopal (3) uses 'New Bollywood' as an aesthetic category and sees it as the phase of genre diversification in the Hindi film industry. Although I borrow the term from her, I go beyond her usage of the term to mark an aesthetic shift and attempt to examine the material practices of the disaggregation of the kind of products that the Production Houses are invested in. Thus, accepting her usage, I argue that genre diversification and the resultant new aesthetic formations are consequences of the reorganization of the industry and try to understand how the material practices of this -reorganized industry create space for diversified aesthetic practices.

Furthermore, the 'New Bollywood' moment is a departure from the idea of 'Bollywood', which when it was coined had a transnational connotation backed by ideas of media convergence and global media flows, in academic as well as in journalistic discourses. 'Bollywood', unlike Hollywood, is often understood as a sensibility, more than just as a film industry. Prasad (7) says that Bollywood plays a pivotal role in articulating definitions of national identity for the figure of the Non-Resident Indian (NRI) because he senses that the 'NRI is increasingly beginning to look like the sole guarantor of Indian identity' in a global arena. Rajadhyakshya (7) marks Bollywood as the arrival of 'a new culture industry'– a bi-product of the growing economic power of diasporic Indians – that thrives on its own narrative, audience and box office economy. More recent scholarship on Bollywood, especially the works of Amit S. Rai and Anustup Basu, is invested in theorizing media beyond the narrative and is attentive to the axes that gives form and consistency to the loose 'assemblages' that define the extra-filmic 'cinema effect' of Bollywood films in India. Basu conceptualizes the period of globalization and new media in India (1991–2004) as the period of cinematic procedures which can be gauged as signs of an impulse towards an 'Advertised modernization', rather than as 'signs of post-colonial India's long gestating engagement with modernity' (92). Rai points out how pleasure from the filmic experience is temporally extended beyond the entire plot of the film and into a secondary level of clips which percolate through devices employed to experience them (216).

This work is situated in a similar field of enquiry, but I argue that the emergence of 'New Bollywood' is a distinct moment within the Hindi Film Industry, which is not just about the global or the extra filmic attributes of Hindi films, but is about the shifts that occurred with the development of a corporate led Production House culture and the advent of multiplexes since 2000 in terms of aesthetics, content, production, circulation and consumption practices. Punathambekar's media industry analysis (14) gives us a very good idea of the manner in which media strategists seek to maximize their profits off a single media product through a capillary infiltration of all dimensions of media. He observes that a phenomenon like this indicates the new social and institutional arrangements and adaptations that theories of globalization are yet to take into account (14). Also Tejaswini Ganti's decade-long ethnography of the Bombay film industry of the late 1990s (2012) gives us a first-hand idea of how visions of 'product creation and management' come about on the ground and then are carried forth by an arsenal of workers starting from corporate heads, producers to actors to distributors to publicists and marketers to multiplex owners. Bose (2006) elaborates how film entertainment in India is no longer just an 'artistic or creative enterprise', but the rapid convergence of various media like – home video, satellite television, radio, internet, animation and gaming, which determines the success or failure of films. Drawing upon these works, elaborating upon the implications of these arguments and substantiating it with my research, I argue that in the period from 2000 to the contemporary, the Hindi film industry scenario has transformed leading to a newer production logic and disaggregation of products and segmentation of audiences. This is the 'New Bollywood' moment, which I mark from 2000 onwards, and attempt to understand the new formations of the industry and its operational forms under the 'Production House' model. In the following sections of this article, I will discuss various aspects of the Production House culture in 'New Bollywood'.

Marketing and exhibition of films in New Bollywood

In the Production House culture, a film is a brand, which, in order to acquire salience in the audience's mind amidst many of its kind, needs marketing processes like promotion, publicity and advertising. Currently promotion seems like the most important function of film marketing. Earlier the parameter of success was the number of days a film ran in a theatre. That was the era of silver jubilees, golden jubilees and diamond jubilees; but today, a film's box office collection over the first weekend decides its fate. Trade experts expect a film to do 50–60% business over the opening weekend, good reviews from film critics notwithstanding.[2] Thus, more and more production houses wish to adopt 'out-of-the-box' marketing strategies to cut through the clutter in a highly competitive space. For example, to promote *Paan Singh Tomar* (2010), the film's producers strung up INR 3.5 lakhs cash on a hoarding in Juhu area in Mumbai.[3]

However, sometimes even with big marketing, promotion budgets and innovative promotional planning, certain films seem to do well while others don't, for example, *Kurbaan* (2009) which in spite of a controversial bare back poster of Kareena Kapoor with Saif Ali Khan did not fare well. The paid previews of the film reportedly earned UTV Motion Pictures only INR 1 crore from 500 shows. The film was reportedly made with a budget of INR 50 crores, excluding the marketing budget. On the other hand, *Chennai Express* (2013) was apparently made at INR 115 crores and promoted with some more and it seems to have made INR 396 crore for the producers at the box office. *Chennai Express* is always touted as a case of marketing genius in the industry – the release of video games, posters in different languages, offering snacks with local flavour wherever it was screened, product/costume endorsements by actors and Shah Rukh Khan was even spotted at a fashion show walking the ramp, an alien territory for him. The level of involvement of a production house in a film's marketing depends on whether it produces a film entirely as opposed to co-producing or just presenting a film. For example, on *Peepli [Live]*'s success Amir Khan (Actor-Producer) said in an interview with *Business Standard*.[4]

> We had to establish in our promotions that it is from Aamir Khan Productions so that the trust and faith that I have earned so far would get it noticed. Second, we had to allow the film's matter to speak for itself. There are films which are watched by fans because of a star actor or director. But the hook for films like*Peepli [Live]* has to be the plot. So, promos become the backbone of the films' marketing. That is where UTV, the co-producer, stepped in.

One of the striking features of film marketing that I was told about by professionals from different Production Houses[5] is that apparently marketing of a film is not limited to its audiences. A film needs to be marketed to external stakeholders too within the industry to ensure recovery of costs, even before the film releases, through the sale of satellite, home video and music rights in international and domestic markets. Sunil Doshi (Celebrity Manager) explains the role of promotion thus[6]:

> We have 52 weeks and there are many films releasing every week. So every week people are bombarded with choices, and whenever there are choices, there is an inclination towards the popular choice. In making a cinema which is author led, for example *Aankhon Dekhi* (2013), Rajat Kapoor (the Director) has never paid attention to the audience's taste which is populist. He is not David Dhawan who will think about 'Taali kahan bajegi' (where will I get claps) while scripting. He has managed to get publicity within the sensibility he is catering to; but it becomes a larger business when one is out in the theatre; there it is a rat race. There is the belief that who can shout the loudest, and if you don't your film is doomed to fail.

It is interesting to also note how marketing a film for its box office performance becomes essential in the multiplex regime of New Bollywood. With more and more multiplexes in operation across India, Indian film producers perceive their audiences differently and segment their films accordingly, in order to offer a venue for niche middle-class-oriented films in a range of styles not previously viable with an idea of a mass public. This is a characteristic of the shifts that occurred in distribution and exhibition techniques with the emergence of functions like programming in multiplexes which entail screen allotment, time slotting, etc. Ansh Kapoor, Programming head of Fun Cinemas, Mumbai talked about how for films that are touted as Blockbusters, programming is very simple vis-à-vis other films. He says:[7]

> There are blockbuster films with a big star cast e.g. *Kick* (2014) which are universally appealing and which will be given all screens and all time slots across theatres. But then there are other films which cast less popular actors, or which have a non-commercial storyline or Hollywood films, for which we need to decide the number of screens and time slots based on our research on audience type, audience behavior, footfall pattern, etc.

It is important to note, in the statement above, the nexus that is there between New Bollywood's distribution mechanism and a multiplex company like PVR or Cinemax. Film distribution, as a function, used to be independent of film production till the Production Houses in New Bollywood created distribution units or divisions within the same corporation, in order to distribute films made by themselves and even to distribute films that they acquire from independent producers. However, what happens, as a result of this is that the films that get made independent of the Production Houses have to not only generate funds to make a film and promote/market it, but also struggle to get it distributed and get a prime slot for exhibition in multiplexes. PVR Movies claim that with PVR Director's Rare, a subsidiary exhibition unit of PVR Movies, they have created an alternative exhibition space to promote 'Indie' films (films produced and distributed independently by the maker/s without involving any of the Production Houses) in order to promote 'a new cinematic culture'. However, the pricing of the tickets in this space is not affordable by one and all (more than INR 1500 per ticket). The filmmaker also has to pay PVR to exhibit in this space. Manav Kaul (Actor-Director) who made *Hansa* (2012), which was released in PVR Director's Rare, shared[8]:

> PVR called me a day before my film was going to release at PVR Director's Rare and said that I am supposed to pay 1 lac Rupees and only then they can send the DCP (the digital hard drive) for screening and apparently it is written in the form which I didn't read before and I had almost given up.

In the light of this, one needs to really question whether there is any alternative space for films that are not produced, distributed and exhibited by the structures of New Bollywood. Siddharth Roy Kapoor (Erstwhile MD and CEO, Disney India) said[9]

> We don't want 13 sub distributors across the country doing what they want with our films. We may sell and sometimes we may not, but we want the ability to have a production and distribution set up within our own system, and market our films ourselves to create a demand amongst audience which will make sure that the exhibitors exhibit them.

Stardom

'No content, big star' and 'great content, no star' – in both scenarios, a New Bollywood film runs the risk of sinking, 'unless', like Manish Hariprasad (Ex-Marketing Head of Red Chillies Entertainment) jokes,[10] 'there is Salman Khan!' The Production Houses have in a way opened up avenues for newer scripts, newer directors and even lower budget films[11]; however, they still haven't been open to the idea of an unknown star cast. The lesser known the cast, the higher is the risk of failure, even with a great script.

Independent films with lesser budgets and new actors, yet great scripts may flop at the box office because of low visibility and odd time slots which would be the consequence of no P&A (Publicity and Advertisement) budget. In the rat race of many films releasing every week, the maximum time a film gets to make an impact and earn profit is just the first weekend of its release, where the competition is not about the content of the film but about the buzz created before its release, which is a bi-product of the P&A budget on that film. More buzz and a more conducive timeslot ensures more footfall and both of these depend on the popularity of the star/s acting in the films. Sometimes, a star may just lend his name to the film or appear in a song or just promote or present the film, to provide credibility to it. Amitabha Sinha (Cinematographer/Producer) sums up this phenomenon thus[12]:

> I make a product (It really hurts me to use the word 'product' for films but I have to do it in today's day and age in the industry) to the best of my knowledge, ability, skill, awareness, preparedness, and then I use any of these social items e.g. Amir Khan to make my target group (again audiences are called that now-a-days) comfortable. Now that films are being driven into that notion of a product, then I would rather make the best product and get the best face

to endorse it and find some sort of a synergy between the two so that the audience is hopeful of a believable product.

Thus, stars are the brand ambassadors of the films that they 'endorse' as brands and hence stardom in New Bollywood is an important aspect that determines the success or failure of the film.

Furthermore, new comers are made stars by the Production Houses. Every big Production Houses likes a Yash Raj Films or Dharma Productions, etc. has a roster of actors under contractual bonds who are managed by its in-house Talent Management division. In the films produced by it, it will use these actors in lead roles as per the contract. But for the rest of the cast they will hire casting directors to do the job of casting. An actor who is on one Production House's roster cannot work outside that Production House's control till the contract expires. Actors too see this as an opportunity to get visibility in an otherwise cluttered industry. Some Production Houses sign such exclusive contracts with writers and directors too. Mr Jogi (Casting Director for films like *Vicky Donor*, 2012 and *Madras Cafe*, 2013, amongst others) mentions[13]:

> Once an actor gets noticed after giving 2–3 hits, the production houses rope them in. And then when they call us for discussing the casting brief vis-à-vis the script, they would tell us that this actor has already been signed by us, so he has to play the lead. Sometimes it is strange because as a person who is skilled to cast people as per roles, you know that this guy or girl isn't going to fit that character at all. Now it is your call, either you do it because credits will show your name or you decide not to.

Understanding all of this will get easier once we try to understand the one specific production logic which, I argue, has been introduced by the Production House culture and which turned it around for these corporations to control the Hindi film industry and the way it functions today.

The 'Portfolio Approach' in New Bollywood

The portfolio approach indicates how New Bollywood functions with its new circuits and strategies, its new production, circulation and consumption logics within the framework of a corporatized entity. This approach characterizes the proliferation of Hindi films that are aesthetically and content-wise different from the films that were made in the previous decades. It is using this approach that the production houses strategize to balance the scales of production not only through the production of big, medium and small budget films but also through the creation of subsidiary production units within their brand. For example, with the creation of ALT Entertainment in 2010 as a subsidiary body of Balaji Motion Pictures, Ekta Kapoor could diversify into different genres of films which could be made in smaller budgets, e.g. *Love Sex Aur Dhoka* (2010), *Ragini MMS/Ragini MMS2* (2011/2014), *Ek Thi Dayan* (2013), etc. In the next section, I attempt to explain how this approach could have emerged.

In the early 2000s, a few small yet interesting films, made by new or unknown filmmakers without any known big production house producing or distributing it, suddenly received critical acclaim and a certain box office acknowledgement, for example, films like *Haasil* (by Tigmanshu Dhulia), *Pinjar* (Chandraprakash Dwivedi), *Hazaron Khwahishein Aisi* (Sudhir Mishra), all made in 2003; *Maqbool* (Vishal Bhardwaj),[14] *Ab Tak Chappan* (Shimit Amin), *Ek Hasina Thi* (Sriram Raghavan) made in 2004; *Iqbal* (Nagesh Kukunoor), *Being Cyrus*

(Homi Adjania) made in 2005; and *Khosla Ka Ghosla* (Dibaker Banerjee), made in 2006. These were all film-makers who were not from the Bombay film fraternity or even from Bombay itself, but were trying to find their feet in the industry and these films were mostly independently produced. But they were made because there seemed to be a certain kind of belief amongst these makers in their own ability and the story they wanted to tell. Dibaker Banerjee mentions[15] that he didn't even try to get Bollywood to support his first film (*Khosla Ka Ghosla*). He had a 'certain confidence coming from an established background' and being from outside the industry he didn't have any baggage, and so he 'brought a fresh approach to film making' and though his film didn't get noticed in the beginning, he 'didn't get fazed by that' because he believed in his craft and 'gradually it got a cult status'.

This happened not by design but by accident, but suddenly it opened up a new business opportunity for New Bollywood, where subsidiary production units were created within the Production Houses to produce or co-produce small budget films alongside big blockbusters, different in aesthetics and content. Disney UTV started UTV Spotboy in 2007 and co-produced films like *Dev D* (2009), *Udaan* (2010), *No One Killed Jessica* (2011), *7 Khoon Maaf* (2011), etc., and produced *Paan Singh Tomar* (2010);Balaji started Alt Entertainment in 2010 and co-produced *Love Sex Aur Dhoka* (2010), *Shor in the City* (2011), *Ragini MMS* (2011), *The Dirty Picture* (2011), *Ek Thi Daayan* (2013), *Ragini MMS 2* (2014); Viacom 18 started Tipping Point Films in 2011 and co-produced *Shaitan* (2011) and YRF started Y-Films in the same year and produced *Luv Ka The End* (2011) and *Mujhse Fraaandship Karoge* (2011) and also co-produced *Mere Dad Ki Maruti* (2013)

Today the portfolio approach in New Bollywood has led to the production of film like *Aamir*(2008), *A Wednesday* (2008), *Oye Lucky Lucky Oye* (2008) by UTV Motion Pictures, *Rocket Singh: Salesman of the Year* (2009) by YRF, *Luck By Chance* (2009) by Excel entertainment and Reliance Entertainment, *Peepli [Live]* (2010) by Aamir Khan Productions and UTV Motion Pictures, etc. Interestingly, in popular discourse the creation of these subsidiary production units by big production houses has mostly been portrayed as an attempt on the part of the Hindi film industry to respond to changing youth culture and the attempt of the industry to cater to a 'different' section of the audience with different tastes in film viewing. However, I understand it as actually a commercially viable strategy as per the corporate logic of New Bollywood, which is centrally concerned with segmenting its own products. According to Siddharth Roy Kapoor, (MD for Disney UTV in India):[16]

> Today the stakes are getting higher; the financials involved are way higher, the numbers are very big. So it is only the corporations who can afford to fund and release films and we follow the slate model that helps us to even out profits and losses because we make 8–12 films a year, and we do have a decent track record too. On the other hand, if one has to make one individual film at that scale, there are chances of being completely wiped out, which is why individual producers are always looking to co-produce with a studio these days.

This is the reason why independent Hindi ('Hindie') films like *Miss Lovely* (2012) by Oshim Ahluwalia, *Hansa* (2012) by Manav Kaul, *Peddlers* (2012) by Vasan Bala, *Aankhon Dekhi* (2013) by Rajat Kapoor, *etc.* don't manage to get a theatrical release and even if some of them manage to get released, they don't survive at the box office or get noticed by the audience. Such films are vying for the same space as the small budget films produced, promoted and distributed by the Production Houses. Consequently, while these films circulate within scholarly discourses and film festival circuits they fail to get incorporated within New Bollywood, even in the category of 'different cinema' encouraged and supported by the industry's portfolio approach. Ironically, in the absence of any 'parallel cinema' movement, these 'Hindie' films do not have either the cohesiveness or the reputation of being an alternative and a challenge that New-Wave cinema represented in the 1970s. At the same time, since they are not part of the mainstream's portfolio production structure, they do not have the kind of visibility of a different cinema that New Bollywood also wants to back.

Independent cinema and New Bollywood

As outlined in the previous section, New Bollywood is interested in a particular kind of 'indie' cinema, and increasingly we are seeing New Bollywood support some of these indie/Hindie films. These 'Hindie' films are experimental in nature with no big stars, realist scripts, shoe string budgets and no backup from the industry during production and they still manage to survive within the context of and the domination of the market by New Bollywood, which most of the film-makers feel would have been next to impossible in the Hindi film circuit in the 90s. In a scenario dominated by New Bollywood, 'Hindie' films use different pressure tactics on the Production Houses for either acquisition or presentation or distribution. These films try different kinds of strategies to address the politics of release structure in New Bollywood, the most common and effective being the film festival route.

These Hindie films get circulated amongst niche audiences through various national and international film festivals, which in turn help them garner visibility and gain cultural capital, and with the buzz that gets created, these films also hope to get noticed by the producers and distributors of New Bollywood and get picked up. Films like *Ship of Theseus* (2012), *Lunch Box* (2013), *Filmistaan* (2013), *Margarita with a Straw* (2014), etc. followed the same route to be distributed and presented by New Bollywood's Production Houses. Kalki Koechlin (actor/writer) who acted in the film *Margarita with a Straw* says:[17]

> Now independent filmmakers are routing at festivals, to get noticed at festivals. My film *Margarita with a Straw* is about disability and sexuality, but here people who are disabled can't have sex you know (laughs). When Shonali (Bose, the Director) came with the script I loved it and we went ahead and made it on a shoestring budget. So once we managed to rope in Studio 18 (A production House of Viacom Network), they wanted us to go to the festivals to get some international critical buzz so they could then promote and release it.

Allan McAlex, Executive Producer and Co-founder of a Line Production company in Mumbai named *Jar Pictures* explained this best when he talked about the International film festival circuit and how it works. He says[18], 'We use festivals just as a platform to get our film noticed and distributed in the international market and not just as festival films (which are seen as art house films). Festivals are just platforms to launch, for visibility'.

International co-production and collaboration is yet another technique used by independent film producers to minimize risk of loss and also to get noticed in New Bollywood. If these films get co-produced by many individual producers and production companies nationally and internationally, they get talked about and if they seem in sync with New Bollywood's low budget films, aesthetically and otherwise, there is a chance of them being picked up, as the burden of loss gets shared.

Thus, today, even New Bollywood is keeping an eye out for these Hindie films in the film festival circuits, and the Hindie film-makers also need the industry to promote and distribute their films. However, it is also interesting that once these filmmakers manage a theatrical release for their films, they do not go gung-ho about the critical acclaim and festival recognitions that their films have received, because they do not want to be perceived as art house films. The distributors then take over and decide on the promotional materials (poster, trailer, etc.) that would work best for these films so as to bring them to the notice of the target audiences for these films.

Phantomization and New Bollywood

The 'Hindie' films of the 2000s actually owe their co-existence alongside mainstream cinema to a wave that Anurag Kashyap (Writer, Director) brought about, and any discussion on contemporary Hindie films will be incomplete without spending some time on Kashyap. While the Production House culture was being fostered in New Bollywood, a simultaneous phenomenon was occurring outside of New Bollywood, which I am calling *Phantomization*[19], marked by the emergence of an 'alternative' style of storytelling by Anurag Kashyap. Kashyap entered the film scene with a completely different set of films like *Paanch* (2003), *Black Friday* (2007) and *No Smoking* (2007) which actually didn't do well at the Box Office at all. However, after *Dev D* (2009), which did well both in terms of critical acclaim and audience reception at the box office, he began to get noticed and support from the industry, which he used to launch himself as an 'alternative' filmmaker within the industry. However, Kashyap himself never considers himself 'alternative'; it was the industry that tagged him 'Alternative' or 'Tarantino-esque'. He jokes, 'I believe my work has always been and still is very mainstream; only I was way ahead of the industry then to know what mainstream actually is'[20]. He set up Phantom Films, in 2011 as a 'Directors' House'[21] and as an alternative structure to the big Production Houses to open up opportunities for newer directors, writers and actors through a process of 'mentoring' and collaboration to foster this so called 'alternative movement', which he believes is more about a 'different sensibility'. Collaborations could be international or national, and between individuals or with film companies. Kashyap is also very serious about his mentoring model, wherein he provides opportunities to film school graduates or aspirant filmmakers to take a shot at filmmaking, where they fund and handhold the mentees to shoot short films, documentaries and trailers, etc. Phantom Films itself is an outcome of a similar attempt of mentoring and collaboration when Vikas Bahl and Kashyap showed interest in co-producing new comer Vikramaditya Motwane's film *Udaan* in 2010.

Thus, Phantomization in New Bollywood is a crucial phase that interestingly brings about a certain kind of production logic, filmmaking style and sensibility in films which were once termed 'Fringe Cinema' (Mazumdar 198).[22] However, today this is the cinema that, although different in its aesthetics and content which (as Mazumdar points out) disrupts the 'visual culture of brightness' and sculpts an alternative space that is 'dark, melancholic and dystopic' (ibid) is gradually becoming a part of the mainstream in New Bollywood, even in the way it is produced, marketed and distributed, which Kashyap claims to have foreseen. Kashyap admits that he loves to make dark cinema because 'our lives are dark, we are dark; so the cinema that we make needs to reflect that dark'.[23] Kashyap himself has gained currency in New Bollywood because of the cultural capital he gained at Cannes and his collaborative ventures with European film-makers. If Kashyap attaches his name to a project, the Production Houses don't shy away to co-produce, distribute or present that project, case in point being films like *Lunchbox* (2013) and *Masaan* (2015). Many of these new Hindie film-makers like Neeraj Ghaywan, Vasan Bala, Nitin Kakker etc. have admitted that for people like Anurag (Kashyap) and Dibaker (Banerjee) who decided to stand their ground against the monopoly of the New Bollywood led production and aesthetic logic, there is a space for a story to be told differently and yet make an impact in some sections of society.

However, in my mind Indie films stay truly 'Indie' only in terms of aesthetics, because the moment they are acquired or presented by the Production Houses in New Bollywood, they no longer remain economically indie. Moreover, without Production Houses invading the Hindie realm, the process of production and the product both lose their independent edge. So the issue then is how true the filmmakers can stay to their aesthetics when the economic logic of the Production House culture comes into play. Filmmaker Qaushiq Mukherjee, popularly known as Q, (who likes to call himself an 'Image Jockey') is of the opinion that he makes films for self-expression and for his own audience who he knows will watch it whether or not it is promoted or exhibited. His films are 'neither for the festivals, nor for the multiplexes', because in both these places films are made to cater to the audience's taste, whereas he claims that he gets the audience that knows his taste.[24] Now, in the light of what he has said, can we say that people like Q are staying true to the essence of independent films? However, his latest Bengali horror film *Ludo* (2015) was showcased in the Mumbai Academy of Moving Image (MAMI) Film Festival, 2015; it won best film at the Belgrade International Film Festival in Serbia, 2016; and it is also being rewritten in Hindi by a new writer from Phantom Films that Q will be directing. The Hindi film will be distributed by Phantom and exhibited in Multiplexes. When probed on that, Q mentions this to be 'incidental' and that like his previous films, when he was making *Ludo*; he never 'set out with such objectives' (ibid). But the trajectory of *Ludo* seems to illustrate the pattern of incorporation or appropriation of indie films within New Bollywood that I have outlined above.

Conclusion

This corporatized 'New Bollywood' moment has its foundation in the understanding that the business of films is not so much about the image per say, as much as it is about the control of the rights of production; which translate into selling/buying copyrights. It is all about generating profits. The Production Houses controlling the business of film production, distribution and circulation are not exclusively in the business of films alone; the film business is just one vertical of a larger audio-visual industry comprising of the Media and Communications empires, which are omnipresent thus blurring the gap between Hollywood and New Bollywood. Most Production Houses in India, barring Yash Raj Films, Balaji Motion Pictures and Dharma Production, Eros, etc. are actually run by the same parent companies that function in Hollywood and other countries (21st Century Fox, Disney Entertainment, Walt Disney World, Viacom, Sony Pictures, etc.). The Indian subsidiaries are meant to produce and distribute Hindi films and to distribute the Hollywood films made under their banner.

The phenomenon of global media conglomeration which happened in the 90s in Hollywood, took shape in the 2000s here in India, thus opening up opportunities for screen convergence, where a film's earnings are not dependent on just its theatrical exhibition, but also through its release across platforms and screens (Satellite TV, Mobile, home video, etc.). A film reportedly recovers a major portion of its production budget even before its theatrical release through the sale of music and satellite rights for both domestic and international territories, getting advertisers to do in-film placements, etc. and by selling distribution rights to international distributors through sales agents.

Interestingly, the indie film-makers I met have pointed out to me that they could tell the story that they wanted to because they made their films at this moment, and not 15 years ago, when such stories had no space in the Hindi Film Industry. I attribute this to the conglomerate nature of the industry which also happened in the New Bollywood moment in India. It opened up gates for collaboration, domestic and international. Filmmakers like Anurag Kashyap, Dibaker Banerjee, Vishal Bhardwaj, et al. have managed to cross the so called divide through corporate alliances and collaborative projects (of film-making) with the Production Houses. Kanu Behl (Director of *Titli*, 2014) mentioned[25] how Dibaker Banerjee, who was signed on by Yash Raj Films for a 3 film contract, managed to 'slip in' Behl's first film *Titli* along with two of his own films; and *Titli* got made at a 'decent budget' with 'limited interference' from the Production House because of the faith they have on Dibaker's credibility. The Indie movement and the Production Houses are not alternative approaches; they co-exist through navigating the space of New Bollywood with certain pulls and pushes.

Notes

1. Script, stars, music, publicity, etc.
2. *Business Standard*: November 22, 2009. However, some movies do end up garnering finance and reputation through word of mouth publicity after 2–3 weeks of release, but they aren't the 'Box office hits'.
3. http://indiatoday.intoday.in/story/paan-singh-tomar-film-poster/1/175830.html
4. August 30, 2010.
5. Siddharth Roy Kapoor (UTV Disney); Manish Hariprasad (Red Chillies Production); Azeem Dayani (Dharma Productions).
6. In a personal Interview with the author on 16th July, 2014 in Mumbai (India).
7. In a personal Interview with the author on 5th August, 2014 in Mumbai (India).
8. In a personal Interview with the author on 14th March, 2015 in Mumbai (India).
9. In a personal Interview with the author on 31st July, 2014 in Mumbai (India).
10. In a personal Interview with the author on 18th July, 2014 in Mumbai (India).
11. We will discuss such films at length in the next section under 'Portfolio Approach'.
12. In a personal Interview with the author on 14th July, 2014 in Mumbai.
13. In a personal Interview with the author on 30th July, 2014 in Mumbai (India).
14. Bhardwaj's *Maqbool*, when it came out, was not a film that people recognized as one made by a big film-maker. It was one of the films that got noticed and received appreciation slowly.
15. In a personal Interview with the author on 28th October, 2014 in McLeod Ganj (India).
16. In a personal Interview with the author on 31st July, 2014 in Mumbai.
17. In a personal Interview with the author on 30th July, 2014 in Mumbai.
18. In a personal Interview with the author on 6th September, 2015 in Mumbai.
19. I'm using this term to mark a different culture of film production (which I talk about in this section) that seems to be fostered in Anurag Kashyap's production and distribution company *Phantom Films*.
20. In a personal Interview with the author on 23rd July, 2015 in Mumbai.
21. Along with director Vikramaditya Motwane (*Udaan*: 2010; *Lootera*: 2013), producer Madhu Mantena and the former head of UTV Spotboy and director Vikas Bahl (*Chillar Party*: 2011; *Queen*: 2014).

22. In a later piece, Mazumdar further delves into the idea of 'Urban Fringe' with examples of films that disrupt and 'haunt globalization's visual culture of brightness to sculpt an alternative language of space that is dark, melancholic and dystopic' (153).
23. In a personal Interview with the author on 23rd July, 2015 in Mumbai.
24. In a personal Interview with the author on 7th Feb, 2016 in Mumbai.
25. In a personal Interview with the author on 20th December, 2015 in Mumbai.

Acknowledgements

I would like to thank all those I have interviewed for this article and who I have mentioned in my Appendix 1 for enabling me to understand the structures of New Bollywood. This paper would not have seen the light of day without the relentless support of my PhD advisor Prof. Ira Bhaskar (JNU) and critical appreciation by the editors – Dr. Khaleel Malik and Dr. Rajinder Dudrah. I would like to extend my heartfelt gratitude to them and to the reviewers who gave their valuable suggestions, which helped me critically relook at my paper.

Disclosure statement

No potential conflict of interest was reported by the author.

References

Basu, Anustup. 2010. *Bollywood in the Age of New Media: The Geo-televisual Aesthetic*. Edinburgh: Edinburgh University Press.

Bordwell David, Janet Staiger, and Kristin Thompson. *The classical Hollywood cinema: Film Style and Mode of Production to 1960*. Abingdon: Routledge, 1988.

Bordwell David. *The Way Hollywood Tells It: Story and Style in Modern Movies*. Berkeley: University of California Press, 2006.

Bose Derek. *Brand Bollywood: A New Global Entertainment Order*. Thousand Oaks, CA: SAGE, 2006.

Ganti, Tejaswini. 2012. *Producing Bollywood: Inside the Contemporary Hindi Film Industry*. Durham, NC: Duke University Press.

Gopal Sangita. *Conjugations: Marriage and form in New Bollywood Cinema*. Chicago, IL: University of Chicago Press, 2011.

Grainge Paul. *Brand Hollywood: Selling Entertainment in a Global Media Age*. Abingdon: Routledge, 2008.

Mazumdar Ranjani. *Bombay Cinema: An Archive of the City*. Minneapolis: University of Minnesota Press, 2007.

Mazumdar Ranjani. "Friction, Collision, and the Grotesque: The Dystopic Fragments of Bombay Cinema." Ed. Gregory Cowan and Gyan Prakash. *Noir Urbanisms: Dystopic Images of the Modern City*. London: Princeton University Press, 2010. 150–186.

McDonald, Paul, and Janet Wasko. 2008. *The Contemporary Hollywood Film Industry*. Hoboken, NJ: Wiley-Blackwell Publishing Ltd.
Prasad, M. Madhava. "Surviving Bollywood." Ed. Anandam P. Kavoori and Aswin Punathambekared. *Global Bollywood*. New York: New York University Press, 2008. 41–51.
Punathambekar Aswin. *From Bombay to Bollywood: The Making of a Global Media Industry*. New York: NYU Press, 2013.
Rai, Amit S. 2009. *Untimely Bollywood: Globalization and India's New Media Assemblage*. Durham and London: Duke University Press.
Rajadhyaksha, Ashish. 2003. "The 'Bollywoodization' of the Indian Cinema: Cultural Nationalism in a Global Arena." *Inter-Asia Cultural Studies*. 4.1. 25–39.

Appendix 1. List of People Interviewed

Names	Position
Nitesh Tiwari	Writer/Director
R. Balki	Writer/Director/Producer
Amitabha Singh	DOP/Producer
Bejoy Nambiar	Director/Producer
Abhay Chopra	Producer
Swanand Kirkire	Lyricist/Singer
Kamaljeet Negi	DOP
Azeem Dayani	Movie marketing (Dharma)
Sunil Doshi	Celebrity Management (Amitabh Bachchan) and Script sourcing
Gauri Shinde	Writer/Director
Anirban Das	Founder – Director, CAA Kwan
Manish Hariprasad	Head of Marketing – Red Chillies Entertainment
Amit Roy	DOP/Director
T Rajendram	Head of Events – T series
Rajat Kapoor	Writer/Actor/Director/Playwright
Bonny Kapoor	Producer
Sanjay Kapoor	Actor/Producer
Amit Sharma	Writer/Director
Remo D'souza	Choreographer/Director
Jogi	Casting Director
Kalki Koechlin	Actor/Playwright
Siddharth Roy Kapoor	Producer (UTV Disney)
Mukesh Chabbra	Casting Director/Director
Anil Thadani	Distributor
Pradeep Singrole	Independent Filmmaker
Ansh Kapoor	Programming Head, Fun Cinemas
Shoojit Sircar	Writer/Director
Sarthak Dasgupta	Sundance fellow and independent filmmaker
Nitin Kakkar	Director
Atul Kasbekar	Model/Photographer/Celebrity manager
Ashwini Tiwari	Director
Ajai Rai	Line Producer
Bhavna and Sumit Attri	Casting Directors
Dibaker Banerjee	Writer/Director
Manav Kaul	Writer/Director/Actor
Anurag Kashyap	Writer/Director/Actor
Abhinay Deo	Writer/Director
Homi Adjania	Writer/Director
Allan McAlex	Executive Producer
Jason West	Cinematographer
Pan Nalin	Director/Producer
Shanker Raman	Director/Cinematographer
Rafiq Gangjee	CEO/Producer (Cinestaan)
Varun Grover	Writer
Vasan Bala	Director
Neeraj Ghaywan	Director
Q	Director
Kanu Behl	Director

Optimize the contribution of design to innovation performance in Indian SMEs – what roles for culture, tradition, policy and skills?

Simon Bolton, Lawrence Green and Bhavin Kothari

ABSTRACT
This paper examines the historic growth and development of the design sector in India, and evaluates the potential of the industry to contribute to innovation performance as the country's manufacturing sector continues its expansion via a comparative analysis of design policies in advanced economies and those in India, and an evaluation of the performance of design promotional initiatives, the paper identifies lessons that might be incorporated sensitively into the future elaboration of Indian design policy. The paper concludes that design inputs can contribute to both social and economic development (and to innovation performance in both traditional craft and hi-tech manufacturing). However, it also argues that policy to support intelligent growth, diffusion and take-up of design must be attuned to both qualitative issues of culture, diversity and tradition, and to 'harder' issues of location, infrastructure, skills, investment and demand.

Introduction

The relationship between creativity, design and innovation has received increasing scrutiny in both academic and policy circles throughout the past decade. In a discussion triggered by the Cox report (1–10), various strands of thinking and enquiry have emerged. Building from the long-acknowledged link between investment in innovation and growth and competitiveness, several commentators have alluded to the strategic role of design in organizational re-structuring and positioning (Brown 84–93; Furniss 18–23). Others have investigated the theme of design methodologies and approaches and their transferability to non-design settings (Green, Cox and Bitard 268–288), and yet more have addressed the role of design in raising the performance of small- and medium-sized enterprises (Moultrie, Clarkson, and Probert 184–216). Whilst this research has achieved considerable impact on industrial policy-making and firm responses to globalizing markets, it is notable that almost all have been undertaken in highly advanced European and North American economies.

This paper sets out to redress the balance with an investigation of the role of design and design practitioners in enhancing the performance of micro-enterprises and SMEs in the Indian context (ISMEs). Growth rates in the sub-continent have reached enviable proportions in recent years, and at least some of this success can be credited to the design policies and design support agencies that have targeted the improvement of innovation and new product development performance in the SME-based advanced manufacturing sector. The paper builds from a descriptive history of design support policy in both the West (particularly the UK) and India – notably via the visionary inception in the 1950s of the National Institute of Design. It then moves to examine – via analysis of interview data with key design actors and examples of successful innovating manufacturers – the ways in which design methods, approaches, tools and inputs can promote performance and increase competitive advantage. The paper will examine the cross-applicability of design/creativity theories developed in non-South-Asian contexts, and identify the particularities of the contribution of Indian design expertise in generating success for indigenous manufacturing businesses. We focus in particular on the role of culture and cultural and locational diversity in India, and examine how these factors will shape opportunities for, and the role of, design as India's manufacturing and economic growth continues to unfold. We also focus on craft industries and existing technologies (often low-cost technologies) to evaluate the ways in which design can support both economic and social development.

Core aims and structure of the paper

The paper commences by examining the growing body of evidence and commentary relating to the contribution of the creative industries – especially the design sector – to the innovation performance of firms and national economies. It moves on to explore trajectories in policy that have been elaborated as a means of supporting and fostering design, and provides examples and analysis of design promotion initiatives from across the globe. The paper then addresses the ways in which design can be used to leverage competitiveness, and here we address the core issues and questions upon which the study is founded, specifically[1]:

- How and in what ways do the creative industries (CI) and creative practitioners contribute to innovation performance in Indian SMEs (ISMEs), and what is the role of design promotion initiatives in delivering enhanced competitiveness?
- What are the implications of cultural diversity, demographics and regional identity for design-enabled innovation in ISMEs: How is urbanization impacting on the evolution of design ecosystems, and how can design increase capacity to exploit low-cost technologies, craft methods and traditional expertise?

In closing sections, the paper sets out some reflections on both empirical and theoretical components of the study, and considers challenges for the future optimization of design in India. The paper concludes with a review of the factors that are shaping the contribution of design to innovation performance in Indian enterprises, and sets out suggestions for appropriate support policy. Social, economic and industrial development can be aided by intelligent and sensitive application of smart design, though policies to promote such design must be guided by acknowledgement of history, culture and changing realities. In short, further design-related development in India will be required to take account of:

- Implications of the diversity of regional cultures and identities for the role and application of design in Indian ISMEs.
- The influence of urbanisation on design, development and production ecosystems in India.
- Barriers to the adoption and use of design (especially those that hamper delivery of innovation performance in Indian ISMEs).
- Changing practices and applications of (and opportunities for) design in traditional and hi-tech manufacturing.

Creative industries and innovation performance

Today the creative industries (CI) sit at the centre of economic development and growth in both the developed and developing world. They constitute a growing proportion of the economic output and employment of many advanced nations, with contributions to GDP ranging from 2% to 6%, depending, of course, on definitions deployed, and sectors under study (CISAC 24).

Mapping the importance of the CIs to national economic output was pioneered in the late 1990s in the UK, when the Government's Department of Culture, Media and Sport (DCMS) published the 'Creative Industries Mapping Document 1998'. The potential of the CIs to become an engine for economic development and growth was quickly recognized by other national governments, many of which subsequently replicated the format of the UK study. Hong Kong, New Zealand, Singapore and Australia initiated analogous exercises to facilitate measurement of the size and contribution of the creative economy within their own territories (CISAC 20), and each confirmed UK findings of substantial impacts at regional, sector and national levels. At around the same time, and from a sociological perspective, Florida (5–18) contributed ground-breaking work on the links between thriving, cosmopolitan cities and rates of creative enterprise, social tolerance and cultural activity. Florida's studies complemented those of national economic research agencies, and pointed to key factors in regional/city-based sociocultural and creative development.

The Creative Industries were defined by the UK DCMS in 2001 (5) as 'those … which have their origin in individual creativity, skill and talent and which have a potential for wealth and job creation through the generation and exploitation of intellectual property'. It is this definition that is deployed in this paper. We also allude (albeit in an indirect way) to the concept of national systems of innovation, and the factors that affect national performance. Here, we employ Lundvall's notion (1–19) that national innovation systems are characterized by 'the elements and relationships which interact in the production, diffusion and use of new, and economically useful, knowledge … and are either located within or rooted inside the borders of a nation state'.

UK mapping has generated valuable data that has evidenced the contribution of the CIs to the UK economy, and has helped to fuel the development and growth of the creative sector. The recent 'Creative Industries Economic Estimates' study from the UK Government (1–46), helps to illustrate the importance of the CIs to economic performance. From an employment perspective the Creative Economy (CE) had, by 2013, generated 2.62 m jobs: a figure that equates to 1 in 12 of all UK jobs. Between 1997 and 2013 employment in the CE increased from 1.81 m to 2.62 m, equivalent to a rise of 2.3% year-on-year.

The potential value of the CIs has not been missed by developing countries. Commentators, for example, UNCTAD (1–14) and Throsby (66–71) have argued that the value of the CIs to developing nations is linked to their ability to (a) stimulate cultural and social development, such as national identity, social cohesion, preservation of common values and collective institutions and (b) provide a tool for economic growth based on the potential to create employment, generate incomes, earn export revenues and alleviate poverty.

The strength of the data generated by the UK Government's CI Mapping exercises highlights a key dilemma for India. Multiple organizations in the country draw attention to the fact that there is a scarcity of economic data re: the CIs (CISAC 24). This shortage of reliable statistics has resulted in limited systematic analysis and an inability to fully determine the size and contribution of the creative sectors to the Indian economy as a whole. A further underlying challenge resides in weakness in legislative frameworks, in particular, enforcement of copyright (a weakness that has largely been addressed in Western contexts).

These apparent problems are perhaps surprising given the importance, diffusion and ubiquity of Indian culture and its creative products. The Bollywood film industry is a useful case in point. In 2009, Bollywood produced 1,200 feature-length films, compared with 987 productions (in video format) in Nigeria and 694 major films in the United States (UNESCO 9–91). The opportunity for both category and sector growth in the CIs has been emphasized by the Indian National Skill Development Corporation. This body states that out of 21 high-growth sectors with employment expansion opportunities in India, only four are currently in the creative sector domain (textiles and garments; gems and jewellery; handlooms and handicrafts; and media/entertainment/ broadcasting/content creation and animation). Clearly then, there is strong potential for growth throughout the CIs, and the potential contribution of design to the innovation performance of Indian SMEs (both within and outside the CI sector) is substantial.

The promotion of design: Designing policy for competitiveness and beyond

Heskett (71–84) identified a robust link between national competitive performance and the prevalence and quality of design activity. He argues that (effective) design policy enables the promotion and creative use and development of technologies, and that this demonstrably results in the delivery of 'economic advantage by enhancing national competitiveness'. Design and product innovation have long been recognized as key tools for economic growth by progressive governments (this is notable, for example, in Japan, the UK and Germany). A defining characteristic of design – the application of creativity to connect technology and the user – creates a potential for design to act as a critical instrument in fostering and facilitating economic growth at regional and national levels. Acknowledging and underscoring this potential, the achievement of enhanced competitiveness is one of the main rationales that drives the creation and implementation of design promotion policies by governments. National technology and innovation policies have traditionally been the drivers for the creation of design policies and promotion activities. Indeed, Choi, Lim and Evans (79–104) suggest that the most competitive countries 'are working to improve awareness of the importance of design, increasing global competitiveness, and raising people's quality of life'. According to the World Economic Forum Competitiveness index in 2006–2007 (3), 77% of countries at the highest stage of development have had (or retain) design promotion programmes in place. This compares with only 4% of countries located at the lowest stage.

The burgeoning of design policies (typically emerging from industrial policy), that have endorsed the benefits of using design and promoted its role in delivering economic growth and competitive export performance (Do Patrocinio 83–84), has been fuelled in part by (1) the availability of low-cost technologies for production (Velloso 599) and (2) the CI's ability to exploit these. UNCTAD (5–8) argues that these factors have positively impacted on the world economy (especially in developing nations) in the period up to 2008, and – via analysis of comparative international growth rates – it may be argued that this trend has continued to date. There has also been a clear correlation between the use of design policies and export-oriented economic strategies. Another emerging trend is the development of design policies that are focused on more than the creation of economic growth and development: some such policy is now oriented firmly towards the improvement of life for citizens. Lee (16) advocated this shift in favour of more social dimensions by suggesting that effective design policies 'must combine economics, society and the culture of a nation; ranging from increasing exports and nation's competitiveness to a higher quality of life for its citizens'. This movement is reflected in the adoption of strategies with programmatic and broader policy level focus (as opposed to isolated programmes that centre on the linkage of design to industrial policy). The former highlights a more inclusive direction for design policy, one that is targeted at improving national infrastructures, services and systems.

Still relevant today are Bonsiepe's insights re: the development and implementation of design policies in developing countries. Bonsiepe (1–22) highlighted the potential risks of considering craft design as a forerunner to industrial design in developing countries with lower levels technological infrastructure. He has maintained his argument that it is 'misleading' to consider 'industrialization as … a way of overcoming arts and crafts manufacturing methods'. He states that this type of approach often leads to a 'self-inflicted cut-off from development possibilities'. In his pioneering work, Bonsiepe established a series of general rules to support the development and implementation of design policies in developing countries:

- Design should be oriented to available technology and demand;
- Local assessment standards for design should be established;
- Priorities should be based on social benefits and multiplier effects;
- Imported design (and 'know how' and methodologies) should be adapted to local conditions;
- The highest priority should be assigned to training and logistical support.

These principles retain considerable power, especially when viewed in the context of India's national design policy needs: the latter require the encompassing of rural, peri-urban and metropolitan localities and population centres. Indeed, the case of India highlights the importance of engaging with global trends, whilst pointing strongly to the need to tailor policies to support national, regional and local cultures and identities. A 'one-size-fits-all' strategy simply cannot work in such complex settings. Alpay Er (293–307) argued for the need for policies that take into account different development stages within a single country: it can therefore be argued that *'national context'* is paramount in the shaping of design policies (Choi, Lim and Evans 79–104), and that context is influenced by a nation's culture and identity. Potential national design policies are further complicated by the need to simultaneously deal with differing stages of design maturity across the country.

It is clear that India is afforded an opportunity to learn from the experiences of others – both nations and design organizations – with respect to policy design, and the uses for which policy might be employed. However, caution is required. As Maguire and Woodham (19–30) have argued, ineffective infrastructure, education and communication are factors that can lead to failure in the delivery and implementation of design policies. Infrastructure failure has been attributed to poor national distribution of design services, complex delivery structures, duplication of activities between national agencies, saturation of business support programmes and ineffective evaluation processes. Educational failures are deemed to result in an under-skilled workforce and failure to address a lack of capability. This can impact on the growth of urban design industry ecosystems and constrain development of successful (and exemplar) design-based companies and services. Communication failures can result in mixed-messages, weak diffusion of initiatives, and inability to learn (and to diffuse learning) from both success and challenge cases. So, whilst design policy might deliver manifest and manifold benefits, the design of such policy requires sensitivity to: current and evolving needs; existing technologies and skills levels; regional contexts, cultures and industry profiles; communication and diffusion mechanisms; and, the availability and quality of techno-social infrastructures.

Design as tool for competitiveness

Design as a tool for delivering national competitiveness is not new to India. The 1950s was a period of re-evaluation and rebuilding in a newly independent nation. Tasked with rebuilding the country, (and balancing age-old traditions with modern technology and ideas), the Government of India, with the assistance of the Ford Foundation and the Sarabhai family, sought recommendations on a programme of training in design that would (a) serve as an aid to small industries and (b) halt a perceived deterioration in the design and quality of consumer goods. Leading designers Charles and Ray Eames were approached for their advice, and their contribution (along with that of other leading designers and policy actors) resulted in the 'India Report' (1958), a publication that led to the birth of a coordinated approach to design training in India. The report recommended a problem-solving design consciousness that linked learning with actual experience: there was an expectation that such an approach would constitute a bridge between tradition and modernity. The report was underpinned by the values and qualities of a 'good life', and recommended that 'there be close scrutiny of those elements that make up a [desirable] standard of living'. It also advised exploration of the meaning and utility of 'the existing symbols of India'. On the basis of the recommendations of the India Report, the Government established in 1961 (at Ahmedabad), the National Design Institute. This was to be an autonomous body under the aegis of the Department of Industrial Policy and Promotion and the Ministry of Commerce and Industries. Now known as the National Institute of Design, the organization has expanded with additional campuses in Gandhinagar and Bengaluru. There are currently proposals for the initiation of four further branches – a testament to India's commitment to the development of design education.

Historically, Indian companies have relied (in large measure) on designs from external sources. According to the Confederation of Indian Industry (CII 19–26), such companies would employ in-house designers too, but largely as translators of design, and as 'modifiers' of plans to meet with existing production capabilities and local user needs. This approach has arguably restricted the growth and development of design within Indian industry. The 'import' situation continues, to this day, though it is common now for both novel and adaptive design activities in India to be undertaken by in-house designers. In-house design departments are prevalent in companies in the consumer products, automobiles, fashion and accessories, software and hardware, and furniture design sectors. Many young designers elect to work in such in-house departments as they perceive benefits in terms of predictable hours, career paths and opportunities for structure and collaboration. Whilst individual choices are understandable, it can be argued that the emphasis on relatively minor modification activities has contributed to limitation on the understanding of how design might be deployed strategically within organizations (Brown 90–93). Many SME's perceive design to be complex and challenging, particularly when it is recommended as a strategic tool to assist in responding to business challenges. This is problematic: it is precisely in this role that design might deliver greatest value to growth- and new product-oriented smaller firms (Bolton and Green 29–30).

There are parallels in research with UK SMEs that indicate that SMEs experience greater levels of uncertainty and risk-aversion when working on strategic front-end innovation activities (see Figure 1: concept development stage (CDS) activities A and B): such firms report greater confidence when processing rear-end incremental product development activities (Figure 1: CDS activities E and F). In relation to front-end activities (A–C) uncertainty can be attributed to several factors: (i) lack of resources and expertise, (ii) insufficient end-user contact, (iii) the adoption of low risk/incremental strategies, (iv) over familiarity with served markets and (v) irregular engagement in 'genuinely new' product development. Clearly then, there are factors shared across Indian and UK SMEs. Further, for both UK and Indian SMEs, application of design may not constitute a high priority in the face of other pressing business imperatives. As the Design Council ("Designing Demand" 1–8)

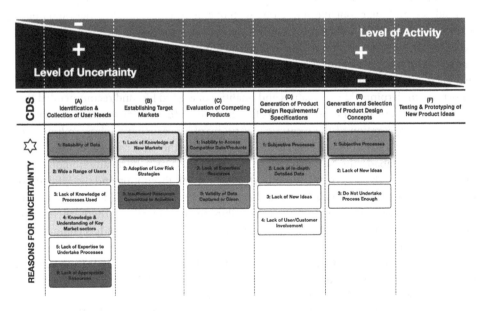

Figure 1. Levels of uncertainty in SME front-end innovation activities (Bolton 165).

suggests, design frequently constitutes a focus for attention in times of affluence, not those of economic squeeze.

As noted above, the power of design is important to developing countries as it founded on an ability to connect technology, creativity and the user. Many in the CIs have realized this potential and have learned how to exploit low-cost technologies. The capacity of design to foster and facilitate change – in combination with its potential as a tool to assimilate technological advancement for quality of life and societal improvement – make it a forceful potential driver for both social development and economic advancement in developing countries. These are recurring objectives in India, ones that lie at the heart of the India Report of 1958.

Moreover, design can be used specifically to address 'technology-stagnation' in developing countries. This is of particular importance given the conventional reliance of Indian companies on imported design and local adaptation. As Indian industry produces greater numbers of original products, the role of design and designers will become more important. The recent inception of the 'India Design Mark' – a celebration of good design – is an initiative that was launched to promote excellence in indigenous design.[2] The adoption of the Mark by the India Design Council attests to the raised profile of design in the county, and authorities are eager to see design embedded as (a) a tool for national competitiveness and (b) a differentiator of exported products and services. Design can also be linked to key Indian export sectors, both traditional and evolving. Such sectors are broad and varied and include, for example: handicrafts, leather items and hand tools; small industry turnkey projects; IT solutions; and, provision of relief supplies (for the UN, etc.)

Opportunities and challenges

As we note earlier, the adoption and performance of design can be adversely affected by ineffective infrastructure, education and communication: individually and combined, these factors can undermine the efficacy of design policies (Maguire and Woodham 19–25). To offset potential challenges, governments (both developed and developing) need to create and maintain a positive and conducive environment for design, and an appropriate supporting infrastructure. Where these factors are in play, design will be well-placed to contribute to the innovation performance of SMEs (CII 95, 96). An opportunity exists for governments to integrate design in core areas of its own service provision, and thus test ideas and provide exemplars – such an approach has been adopted in the UK and elsewhere with the involvement of designers in service development (Arawati, Barker, and Kandampully 170–190). The approach aids in optimizing investments, and in ensuring that services are aligned with citizen's needs (CII 105).

An example of good practice resides in the Design Clinic Scheme, an initiative conceived and operated by the Indian Ministry of Micro-, Small- and Medium-Scale enterprises and National Institute of Design (Development Commissioner India 4–7). The objectives of the Design Clinic scheme are to enhance industry understanding and application of design and innovation, promote design as a value-adding activity, and, to integrate it into the mainstream business and industrial processes of SME's. The scheme addresses a diverse range of products from the very simple to the technically complex, and focuses on micro and small and medium enterprises (MSMEs)' that are vulnerable to business, political or social change.

The Clinic scheme was founded on the basis of lessons from the UK Design Council's 'Designing Demand' programme (Design Council 1–11). The purpose of the latter has been to build capabilities in UK SMEs, and to understand how such firms can use design strategically and effectively within their business. Driven by a 'learning by doing' approach, the programme has successfully enabled businesses to identify how design best meets their aims. It has also supported them in implementing tangible design-enabled projects that are configured to pursue business objectives. The Indian and UK schemes share a common goal of aiding SME manufacturing firms to ascend the value chain: however, despite visible success, a majority of Indian and UK MSMEs still use design only sparingly. This, of course, prompts the question, 'why is this the case'? Analysis of the literature surfaces three key challenges to the adoption of design: ineffective communication (Chiu 187–210); lack of capabilities; and, business strategies that are risk averse (Design Council "Design for Innovation" 9). CII (95–96) indicates that the biggest barrier for Indian businesses in embracing design for innovation is a lack of information. The Confederation finds that businesses are rarely aware of the potential offered by design disciplines: this is connected with a scarcity of economic/performance data and an inability to communicate benefits.

A lack of capability and skilled workers is a fundamental challenge for India. The Indian Design Council (17, 37–43) indicates that design education at school and university level has been recognized as a prime factor in sustaining high-quality design at regional and national level. Currently in India there is poor availability of skilled design professionals. This situation is created in part by the previously stated over-reliance (especially in engineering production) on foreign technical know-how and design. The failure to sufficiently develop indigenous design and development capabilities is caused by lack of investment in design skills – as a result, the Indian market continues to remain flooded with foreign products that in many cases do not meet the aspirations or needs of local consumers (CII 79–94). A shortfall in quality and highly qualified design faculty also exists, and this is both hindering the training of design graduates, and the development of new design institutions in India. There is a common sentiment within the design industry that current design graduates are not well-equipped as a result of a disconnection between syllabi and industry design trends – design education cannot keep up with developments in practice (Furniss 21). The design industry is also in need of support to develop the design management skills of its existing practitioners (Topalian 10–18). From an industry perspective, it is also evident that there is a language and communication problem: business frequently fails to speak the language of design, and designers are unable to connect adequately with business concepts and needs: it is imperative that designers communicate in a language that executives understand (and vice versa) (Bolton and Green 4–10).

According to the Korean Institute of Design Promotion (1), design-related investment in India is amongst the lowest in the world: design is evidently an underused activity in most Indian businesses, and one that is frequently perceived as an expense item reserved for large companies. Traditional Indian SMEs have typically relied on cost innovation strategies, as investments in research have been outwith their capabilities. There is evidence that Indian SME's rely very little on R&D for innovation: both formal and informal manufacturing sectors demonstrate very modest connection with design (CII 98). The development of in-house, adaptive, design capabilities is arguably a poor short-term investment, and symptomatic of a lack of willingness among entrepreneurs to develop markets via the introduction of genuinely novel and innovative product ideas. Product innovation is not typically seen as a vital concern in Indian industry, thus design rarely achieves priority status. Whilst the situation is not so entrenched in the UK, there are parallels in a lack of willingness to engage designers in a strategic role (IDC 44–57).

Despite the challenges, design can be a crucial enabler of innovation performance in SMEs. Current trends in product innovation have blurred the distinctions between the various industrial sectors (IDC 12–36). An effective design promotions strategy/policy can help to improve quality and differentiation, assist creation of world-class products and services, improve business efficiency (and productivity and margins), increase revenues and support increased market share and accelerated growth (CII 100, 101). Design is an important means of generating user-centred innovations, and competitiveness for businesses (Brown 84–91; Martin 1–14), but one that is insufficiently used by SMEs in developed and developing countries. Design is also a fundamental building block of innovation, a critical enabler of competitive industry, and a key pole in the construction of 'livable', sustainable and cohesive communities (CII 105).

There is a growing awareness of the need for more systematic and methodical inclusion of user experience factors in design (Brown 87–93) – such an orientation is underpinned by design-allied competencies in marketing research, consumer behaviour, technology, anthropology and psychology. Moving towards user experience-based approaches will enhance the role of design companies in shaping strategy (rather than merely informing or executing this), and the growing acknowledgement of the value of interaction and service design is helping the discipline to break free from its traditional craft based roots in India, particularly in urban-industrial locations such as Mumbai and Bangalore.

Influence of culture and identity on design and innovation performance

Numerous multinational corporations have attempted to enter the Indian market and have rapidly realized the need to better understand both (a) the Indian consumer and (b) differing regional cultures if they are to meet the needs and aspirations of an increasingly assertive, active and enlightened consumer market (CII 100–105). Some corporations have recognized that successes elsewhere may not translate directly to success in India. Further, some have acknowledged the role that 'indigenous design' can play in blending local technologies and imported components (and vice versa, unifying local needs and imported technologies) (IDC 24).

A key characteristic of India is its cultural pluralism – perhaps not surprising in a nation of such size and history. It is a nation that comprises multiple smaller social groups within a larger society: each maintaining its unique cultural identities, values and practices. Indian culture has been heavily influenced by Dharmic religions, which bring together multifarious traditions, achievements, beliefs, religions, values, cuisines and forms of dress in one nation, a nation that is defined by its kaleidoscope of regional cultures. In a zoning exercise established in 1985, India was described as comprising seven cultural zones (South, South Central, North, North Central, East, North East and West). The Indian Ministry of Culture (http://www.indiaculture.nic.in) undertook the configuration and definitional work with the stated goal 'to strengthen the ancient roots of Indian culture and evolve and enrich composite national culture'. These seven zones reflect the individuality and diversity of India.

Within and across such zones, Indian consumers are starting to display behaviours that have been evolving in advanced capitalist economies: they are becoming more demanding and assertive (Wikström 359-374), confidently pursuing aspirational lifestyle goals. As aspirations change for greater numbers of Indian consumers, design has a potential to facilitate the 'reading' of trends and lead the development of meaningful and sustainable products, thus aiding in driving consumption-led growth. India provides both and an opportunity and challenge for design (Ravi and West 2-28). Diversity (cultural, social and economic) in the range of challenges is so vast that designers must be equipped with appropriate knowledge, skills and flexible learning capacity: these qualities are essential if designers are to enjoy success (Heskett 71-84). Cultural and lifestyle differences – alongside access to technologies and prevailing social conditions – result in forms of demand that can be highly variegated (IDC 44-57). An example here is the bicycle: whilst in developed countries it is uncommon for bicycles to be used to carry loads, in rural India, cycle-based cargo shipment is common. Therefore, designing a bicycle for rural versus urban Indian environments poses different challenges for the designer and manufacturer. Such cultural diversity creates a challenge for design education: the range of design provision and skill sets required by design professionals can be very broad indeed.

To even the casual observer, it is clear that 'craft' is embedded within the culture of Indian design (Finger and Schuler 20; McGuirk *Guardian*). Traditionally, craft practices and practitioners have been considered the initiators of design in India. Textiles have been at the heart of this, as they combine craft and design principles (so too they have been at the centre of the transition from rural to urban-based manufacturing). Many design disciplines still refer back to craft practices to understand the skill requirements of designers. Crafts account for 15 to 20% of the India's manufacturing workforce, and contribute 8% of GDP in manufacturing. However, craft remains a neglected area in development efforts in India (CII 9-16). Responding to local needs through new product innovation is an important requirement (IDC 44-57): craft-based industries have the potential to reinvigorate local (rurally based) trades, occupations that are often abandoned in favour of employment in cities (IDC 37-43, 52). For example, local toy and doll industries with appropriate design and marketing inputs could be used to generate sustainable employment in rural and semi-urban areas. The Confederation of Indian Industry (96-106) argues that design has the potential to leverage indigenous manufacturing and to encourage exports of labour-intensive manufacturing. However, collaborations are often difficult for small-scale craft-based industries. There are examples of success though: one such is the Co-optex initiative with Fabindia, an Indian chain-store retailing garments, furnishings, fabrics and ethnic products that are handmade by approximately 40,000 craftspeople across rural India (Wood 89-100). Collaborating with the National Institute of Design, the partnership helped to combine craft skills (Dastakar craftspeople) with design in order to introduce a new product range that helped to revitalize an ailing brand.

In France, India and Sweden, consumers frequently favour a design style that is reflective of their unique cultural characteristics, this is often referred to as a reflecting a national design identity (National Design Competitiveness Report 1-16). Previous research (Douglas and Nijssen 621-642; Suh and Kwon 663-680; Doyle et al. 419-442) has established the importance of national design identities in achieving competitive advantage in international markets. Dawson et al. (395) argue for the importance of regional and national product identities, stating that 'the country of origin of a product has a significant bearing on the consumer buying decision'. According to the Korea Institute of Design Promotion (6), Italy is rated as having the world's most effective national design identity. Through international promotion it has achieved recognition of national craftwork skills across a range of sectors, developed the value of design, and massively enhanced national brand equity. 'Make in India', is a national government programme (launched by the current Prime Minister), that aims to transform India into a global manufacturing hub. Employing Dawson et al.'s (393–404) '*country of origin* principles' the programme is designed to promote India as a provider of innovative manufacture. The initiative encourages the use of design innovation to (a) help explore new product development opportunities, (b) support new market creation, (c) trigger go-to-market mechanisms for new ideas, and (d) underpin development of product-service ecosystems.

Reflections – Challenges for the future optimization of design

Our comparative review of policy and design industry development literatures, and our research with respect to a spectrum of design promotion initiatives, highlighted four complex and inter-leaving factors/themes that are explicitly (and sometimes more subtly) shaping the contribution of design to the innovation performance of Indian SMEs.

Interviews were conducted with the Chief Coordinator of the MSME Design Clinic scheme from NID, Mr. Jitendra Rajput and regional coordinators, Purindar Dutta and Ashok Mondal. In addition, two designers that are engaged to work on the MSME projects were interviewed. During interviews, issues addressed included: (1) how and why do cultural issues (such as Indian identity, regional characteristics) impact on the role and use of design in India; (2) in what ways and why do urban locations impact on the take-up and use of design; (3) why have specific geographic locations (Pune, Mumbai, Bangalore, New Delhi) become key design powerhouses; (4) what skills impact on the adoption and use of design in Indian industry; and, (5) how is India balancing craft-based design, societally driven design and consumer-driven design? The interview exercise also permitted more profound contextualization of early, literature-based and country-comparison findings and sensitization to evolving realities of current design-innovation-business relationships in India. The four key themes relate to (a) implications of regional cultures for the take up of design, (b) influence of ubanization on the design infrastructure, (c) design education and the alignment of business-design expectations, and (d) changing practices in the application of design (across various sectors).

Impact of regional culture(s) and traditions on the role and use of design in Indian SMEs

Historically and culturally, the roots of Indian design activities can be found in traditional craft practices (CII 7–15). 'latent design' practice emerged from established craft practices that placed emphasis on form and aesthetics. A vast array of different forms of craft products are inextricably linked to the rural economy and its sociocultural milieu (differentiated according to regional location) (IDC 27, 35). At a cultural level, the past and present are linked by craft in India. Some commentators assert that rural crafts constitute a last bastion against loss of identity among various culture groups. Crafts, when understood properly and developed with sensitivity, can connect the rural economy with the modern urban economy to great commercial (and social success). For example, the design-led firm, 'Hidesign' uses full grained leather that is vegetable tanned via traditional methods of soaking hides for

40 days in the extracts of barks and seeds, then hand rubbed with dyes to improve grain visibility and impart a strong and natural look. These traditional high-quality materials are then fused with contemporary design skills to produce items, that whilst exclusive, are reflective of an Indian national design identity. Hidesign embodies the precept of the Design Clinic scheme team that 'crafts are yesterday's innovations and therefore the foundations for tomorrow's innovations'. The Hidesign example provides a powerful pointer to possible future innovating collaborations (ones that fuse tradition with cutting-edge design and techniques). However, Mr. Dutta and Mr. Mondal, regional Design Clinic officers opine that there are currently few well-established Indian brands that emanate from traditional practices (unlike Italy that has multitude of global luxury brands that originate from small regional enterprises).

The potential is evident nonetheless. Deep Kapuria, Chairman, CII Trade Fairs Council stated in 2013 that the Indian MSME sector provides excellent opportunities for both self-employment and wage-employment outside the agricultural sector, and that it contributes in building an inclusive and sustainable society in myriad ways via creation of non-farm livelihoods at low cost, providing balanced regional development, enhancing gender and social balance, and delivering environmentally sustainable development. Where craft-based MSMEs are able to fuse traditional making skills and materials with strong design sensibilities, both export and aspirational home markets may come within reach.

Impact of urbanisation on design ecosystems in India

The decline of India's agricultural sectors (in terms of contribution to GDP) commenced in 1941 as the percentage contribution of the secondary sector increased. In addition to partition-fuelled migration in 1947, economic/productive re-balancing resulted contributed to the rapid growth of the four metropolitan cities of Kolkata, Delhi, Mumbai and Chennai. During the period up to 1980, with a goal of achieving a self-reliant socialism, the Indian Government had adopted centralised planning, restrictive investment strategies and a highly regulated approach to private sector business operations. These policies helped to drive the growth of public sector, which resulted in the rapid development of public transport, roads, water supply, electricity and rural and urban infrastructure. However, charges of poor productivity in the public sector, alongside political and policy shifts, saw the emergence in the 1990s of private-sector driven growth, diffusion of new technologies, increasing living standards, and increasing wages in urban areas. These socio-economic shifts culminated in the development of a new 5 year plan in 2007, one that focused on leveraging urbanization to drive the further economic development of the nation.

Although design awareness has been seen to be unfolding both in rural and urban contexts, design in India is frequently closely linked with urban ecosystems, wherein it is deployed as a bridge between local craft producers, traditional engineering/manufacturing companies and new high-tech operators – entities that are often independent of each other. Essentially, the growth of design in India can be linked to urbanization, and the Indian design industry is predominately situated in four key urban centres, namely Bangalore, Mumbai, Delhi and Pune (CII 14). The growth of design in these cities is not uniform, though some driver factors are common across the territories.

Bangalore evolved into a manufacturing hub for public sector heavy industries (aerospace, telecommunications, machine tools), space and defence following independence.

Its recent success has been due to its focused concentration on software services (enabled via economic liberalization) and the city has become a main home to India's information technology industry. Mumbai, known as the gateway to India, is a major port and its economy in the period up to the 1980s, was heavily based on textiles and shipping. In recent decades (again, following liberalization and encouragement to private enterprise), the city has become a leading finance and IT centre. It has also established itself as a major cultural centre, due in large part to the explosion of Bollywood, and has become a key creative and media centre. Pune is a city known for its manufacturing and automobile industries, and is recognized as a location for prestigious research institutes for information technology (IT), education, management and training. These capabilities and expert clusters help to attract migrants, students and professionals from India, South East Asia, the Middle East, and Africa. Pune is the fastest growing city in the Asia-Pacific region and is ranked 145th in the 'Mercer 2015 Quality of Living' listings. It is also ranked second in India, just behind Hyderabad, on quality of life indicators. Delhi's urbanisation is perhaps less remarkable, as the city has for centuries been a trading centre at the heart of several key trade routes. In recent times, Delhi has benefited from the existence of a large consumer market, the availability of skilled labour and the presence of a major retail industry. This combination has been important in attracting foreign investment, especially in the consumer market domain.

In addition, these urban areas have industry clusters that are perceived, in general, to be highly receptive to design inputs and to be open to the adoption of design readily, as a result of the close proximity between manufacturing companies, design promotion agencies and design studios. This situation has led to the emergence of 'design hubs' around constellations of sustainable businesses and in existing commercial areas (CII 13, 14). Another contributing factor in urban areas has been the role of design education in helping to sensitize industry actors to the benefits of design, and encouraging them to engage with a ready supply of proven design talent. The availability of designers, access to technical personnel, the inception of design initiatives, the availability of design promotional intermediaries, and local demand for 'design-enabled' or design-rich products has, in effect, provided fertile ground for the flourishing of urban design ecosystems.

Common to all these centres is that they have brought together (informally and formally) groups of educators, designers, design agencies and industry partners in interconnected and concentrated networks. There is a parallel with the UK here, wherein the design economy has a strong concentration in London and the South East of England (though concentration in the UK is nominally organic rather than deliberate) (Design Council "Design Economy" 42, 52, 53). In India, the explosion of mobile broadband has driven the growth in media and graphic design disciplines (CII 35, 45). Delhi leads in terms of having the greatest number of firms offering graphic design services, closely followed by Bangalore and Pune. Whilst the case for clustering of design businesses is strong, it can also be suggested that concentration is to the disadvantage of businesses located in tier 2 and tier 3 cities. Enterprises in these zones have little proximal design provision and experience difficulty in engaging with design companies (and thus, in appreciating the utility of design) (CII 98, 99).

Pune and Bangalore (CII 13) have become the design powerhouses of India. They can both attribute success in part to their ability to: (1) attract qualified design entrepreneurs (such workers settle as they perceive a freedom to operate in favourable conditions and enjoy access to physical infrastructure); (2) create networks of like-minded entrepreneurs and (3) provide an affordable and high quality lifestyle. In addition both cities have also maximized their pre-existing industrial clusters and are well connected with other main centres in India. According to Jitendra Rajput, Chief Coordinator of the MSME Design Clinic scheme, these locations have become 'obvious choices for designers…to set up their design studios'. Mumbai and New Delhi – the traditional economic powerhouses of the country – can offer some benefits, but lack the lifestyle elements. Ahmedabad and Jaipur are aiming to share the mantel as India's new economic and productive centres, and aspire to match the success of Pune and Bangalore as design centres. Of course, each of these cities is a Tier 1 location. This raises the question (as noted above) of the prospects for design–innovation–business coordination in tier 2 and 3 locations – the question remains, will they benefit from trickle-down or find themselves out in the cold?

Design education and skills, and misalignment of visions and expectations

There is general agreement that India has a dearth of 'good' designers. There is also concern that the regions have a lack of capacity to produce appropriately trained graduates, and further that the expectations of existing designers are frequently unfulfilled. Most CI professionals primarily wish to see their products reach and become successful in the market. However, even though many ISMEs undertake design-led innovation projects (under the aegis of design development programmes), only a small proportion of assignments are currently implemented (IIT Design Manifesto 1–11). For example, the engagement of designers via design clinic schemes has been something of an experiment for Indian micro, small and medium enterprises (MSMEs). Hence, not all projects lead to successful interventions. Whilst awareness of the potential of design is raised amongst MSME leaders, there is frustration for designers as their efforts are appreciated but ultimately shelved. Other incompatibilities and mismatches are in evidence. At present, the payment and credit systems of ISMEs is incompatible with designers' expectations and requirements. In addition, difficulties exist in aligning the aspiration of ISME leaders with that of designers and with Design Clinic Scheme (DCS) objectives (CII 66–70). Unfulfilled expectations are creating dissatisfaction for ISMEs, as the latter accuse designers of 'overselling' quality. Clearly, improved communications and alignment of expectations is required.

Practices and applications re: Design in traditional and contemporary manufacturing

Some (enlightened and engaged) ISMEs are gradually recognizing the importance of design. Whilst most understand its role in relation to cosmetic changes (frequently applied at a later stage of the product development process), only a few comprehend the notion of design as a step-wise process and strategy (Brown 84–93). There has been an increase in awareness and receptiveness since the implementation of the DCS, however this impact is still too small to facilitate realistic measurement. DCS has been evaluated overall as a success, and there is clear evidence of gains for all parties. One finding is that various MSME sectors confront different challenges in the incorporation of design, however, research-intensive and engineering based manufacturers (medical devices, machines tools etc.) appear well-attuned to design-collaboration and have been major participants. Some SMEs have moved towards engagement with design at more fundamental levels or earlier stages of the product and process life cycle, though have recognized the importance of strategic design-based interventions (Acklin 50–60).

Conclusions: Optimizing design for ismes

This paper set out with three key aims: first, to review evidence from an international perspective on the factors that can influence the contribution of design to innovation performance at enterprise and national level; second, to examine the role of design support initiatives in delivering enhanced competitiveness (especially in the contemporary Indian context); and third, to examine the implications of cultural diversity, demographics and regional identity for design-facilitated innovation in Indian SMEs

We can conclude that – from a global perspective – design is recognized as an extremely valuable strategic asset at the highest levels of some of the world's most successful corporations. So too, the utility of design processes is recognized increasingly in progressive and enlightened SMEs. Governments in both advanced and developing economies are eager to highlight design (acknowledging its contribution to growth, GVA and exports), and to this end, many are actively engaged in data collection re: design's impact on trade, and in the roll-out of a range of design-promoting initiatives. Indeed, it can be argued that the international profile of design has never been so strong.

If it can be agreed then, that 'good' design is a desirable asset for any country, sector and enterprise (and for social development too), how might it be possible to optimize the application and embedding of design in the Indian context? India is experiencing rapid growth, and design is just one factor that will facilitate its acceleration. However, it is a factor that faces a unique set of challenges – some highlighted in existing initiatives and some suggested by a survey of developmental activities in parallel economies. First, the orientation to design that is prevalent in India (importation and adaptation) must gradually shift in favour of indigenous design. Second, there is much space to blend traditional craft with contemporary design sensitivities – indeed, India with its rich heritage and culture is uniquely well-placed here. Third, concentration of design, whilst understandable, may starve SMEs in non-primary cities of design-enabled innovation. Fourth, design education is worthy of investment – ensuring that such training is relevant and future focused is essential. Fifth, promotional initiatives must be smart and targeted – raising profile for design, providing innovation success examples, and ensuring alignment of visions (between SME leaders and designers) can lead to greater take-up. Sixth, intelligent and responsive policy can provide an environment in which design can flourish: ensuring that measurable outcomes are in place, and that data are collected systematically will assist in sustaining appropriate policy actions. With attention to these factors, the future for design in India is a bright one – the challenges are not insurmountable and the potential benefits of increased use of design are enormous. The rich cultural heritage of the nation offers unique opportunities for development – it is to be hoped that currently developed nations will presently be casting their gaze to India for lessons in the optimization of design-enabled innovation performance.

Notes

1. Note on Methodology and Approach: this paper contains both theoretical and empirical components, the latter designed primarily to provide verification and validation of some of the themes and findings set out in the text. The main body of the work was constructed on the

basis of an exhaustive review of relevant academic, policy and practitioner/industry literature relating to the contribution of design to firm and sector-level innovation performance. This review has a strongly comparative orientation: we examine the international picture as this has developed over the past 50 years, and track the evolution of some of the key ideas that link design with industrial and economic performance. Beyond this mapping, we focus more directly on the development of thinking (and related policy and industry level responses) in the UK and Indian contexts. Of course, the UK has an established record of data collection with respect to the design sector's inputs to (and impacts on) manufacturing – and more recently services sector – production and consumption. This data have provided a rich resource for researchers, policy-makers and design practitioners, and we timeline trajectories in theorizing and policy-development as these are reflected in industry and design-sector promotional agency reports, the writings of design commentators, contributions in academic journals and in government-sponsored publications. This approach is mirrored in relation to the Indian design sector: whilst there is perhaps less material available here (given relative maturity of the industry), there remains much useful information that can be surveyed. In the case of both comparator countries, the researchers (a) deployed their own knowledge of sources (applying standard bibliographic trawl and select techniques), and (b) engaged with a range of design, academic and policy sector experts to construct a comprehensive map of available and relevant resources. This engagement was particularly effective in surfacing relatively new and grey/industry-internal materials. In addition (and subsequent to), the comparative review, the authors were eager to test some provisional ideas and theories with high-level and expert design sector professionals: this was thought to be particularly important in the fast-developing but highly dispersed Indian design-industry context. To facilitate the harvesting of views, the researchers engaged directly with five expert members of the Indian 'Design Clinic Scheme' Team. This engagement was extremely helpful in refining ideas and in contextualizing, nuancing and enriching both India–UK comparisons, and the paper's overall findings. Each of the experts was asked to comment on the five core themes covered in the paper, and their inputs have ensured that the research and its conclusions more adequately reflect evolving realities in the contemporary Indian context.
2. India Design Mark – Celebrating Good Design: development of a system to identify good design becomes an imperative. It is envisaged that in the long run the India Design Mark will serve as a measure that not only provides better products to the Indian consumer, but will also be a major enabler in helping brands become global as 'Made in India' is supplemented with 'Designed in India'. Provision of the 'India Design Mark' (I-Mark) was initiated by the India Design Council to celebrate good design and to promote the competitiveness of Indian industrial design products.

Acknowledgement

The authors wish to extend their thanks to the anonymous reviewers of this paper, and to the editors of the Special Issue. We are immensely grateful for the thoughtful, considered and constructive comments that have ensured optimization of the document. Any errors that remain in the paper, are of course, the responsibility of the authors alone.

Disclosure statement

No potential conflict of interest was reported by the authors.

References

Acklin, C. "Design-Driven Innovation Process Model." *Design Management Journal* 5.1 (2010): 50–60.

Alpay Er, H. "Development Patterns of Industrial Design in the Third World: A Conceptual Model for Newly Industrialised Countries." *Journal of Design History* 10.3 (1997): 293–307.

Arawati, A., S. Barker, and J. Kandampully. "An Exploratory Study of Service Quality in the Malaysian Public Service Sector." *International Journal of Quality & Reliability Management* 24.2 (2007): 177–190.

Bolton, S.M. *Improving Product Design and Development Performances in SMEs with User Centred Design Activities*. Business School/Centre For International Business and Innovation The Manchester Metropolitan University, UK, (Unpublished PhD thesis), 2013.

Bolton, S., and L. Green. "Maximising the Value of Product Design Innovation: Re-framing and Realiging the Business–Design Relationship." *Economia Creativa* 1.2 (2014): 27–41.

Bonsiepe, G. Development through Design – A working paper prepared for UNIDO at the request of ICSID, UNIDO, United Nations Industrial Development Organisation, Vienna, 1973.

Brown, T. "Design Thinking." *Harvard Business Review* 86.6 (2008): 84–93.

Brown, T. *Change by Design: How Design Thinking Creates New Alternatives for Business and Society*. New York: Harper Collins, 2009.

Chiu, M.L. "An Organizational View of Design Communication in Design Collaboration." *Design Studies* 23.2 (2002): 187–210.

Choi, Y., S. Lim, and M. Evans. "Supporting Design: National Business Support Programmes in the UK and South Korea." *The Design Journal* 15.1 (2012): 79–104.

CISAC. *The Creative Industries + BRICS: Review of the State of the Creative Economy in Brazil, Russia, India and China*. International Confederation of Societies of Authors and Composers [CISAC], Paris, 2014.

Confederation of Indian Industries. *Government Incentives and Schemes for Micro, Small and Medium Enterprises (MSMEs) Towards Export Promotion*. Ministry of Micro, Small and Medium Enterprises. CII, New Delhi, May 2012.

Confederation of Indian Industry, Indian Design Report, 2012.

Cox, G. *The Cox Review of Creativity in Business*. Report for HM Treasury UK Government, London, 2005.

Dawson, K., P. Larsen, G. Cawood, and A. Lewis. "National Product Design Identities." *Creativity and Innovation Management*. 14.4 (2005): 393–404.

Department for Culture, Media and Sport. *Creative Industries Mapping Document 1998*. DCMS, HM Government, UK, 1998.

Department for Culture, Media and Sport. *Creative Industries Mapping Document 2001*. DCMS, HM Government, UK, 2001.

Design Council. *Designing Demand National Evaluation 2007–2012*. London: Eden Partners, 2012.

Design Council. *The Design Economy: The Value of Design to the UK Economy*. Executive Summary. London: Design Council, 2015.

Design Council. *Design for Innovation*. London: Design Council, 2011.

Development Commissioner. "Guidelines – Design Clinic Scheme for Design Expertise to MSME Sector", Government of India, Ministry of Micro, Small and Medium Enterprises, New Delhi, 2010. <http://designclinicsmsme.org/wp-content/uploads/Guideline-DC-MSME07-05-2010.pdf>.

Do Patrocinio, Gabriel Henrique Torres. "The Impact of European Design Policies and Their Implications on the Development of Framework to support Futrue Brazilian Design Policies", Unpublished PhD Thesis, Cranfield University, UK, 2013.
Douglas, S., and E.J. Nijssen. *On the Use of 'Borrowed' Scales In Cross-National Research: A Cautionary Note*. New York: New York University, 2002.
Doyle, P., J. Saunders, and V. Wong. "Competition in Global Markets: A Case Study of American and Japanese Competition in the British Market." *Journal of International Business Studies* 23.3 (1992): 419–442.
Finger, J.M. and P. Schuler, eds. *Poor People's Knowledge: Promoting Intellectual Property in Developing Countries.* Washington: World Bank, 2004.
Florida, R.L. *The Rise of the Creative Class: and How It's Transforming Work, Leisure, Community and Everyday Life*. New York: Basic Books, 2002.
Furniss, L. *Beyond Discipline: Design Practice and Design Education in the 21st Century*. Report for Strategic Creativity Research Lab, Birmingham: Birmingham City University, 2015.
Green, L., D. Cox, and P. Bitard. "Design as a Tool for Innovation." *Innovation Policy Challenges for the 21st Century*. Ed. D. Cox and J. Rigby. London: Routledge, 2012.
Heskett, J. "Creating Economic Value by Design." *International Journal of Design* 3.1 (2008): 71–84.
IIT. "Design Manifesto." Hyderabad: The Department of Design at IIT-Hyderabad, 2014.
Indian Design Council. "Design as a Strategy for a Developing Economy." IIT Bombay (update, 2009), Bombay, 2009.
Korean Institute of Design Promotion. "National Design Competitiveness Report." KIDP, Seoul, 2008.
Lee, S. *Design Policy and Global Network: World Design Forum Proceedings*. Seoul: KIDP and ICSID, 2002.
Lundvall, B.Å., ed. *National Innovation Systems: Towards a Theory of Innovation and Interactive Learning*. London: Pinter, 1992.
McGuirk, J. "How will India design its new identity?" <https://www.theguardian.com/artanddesign/2012/mar/15/india-design-identity-forum-new-delhi> (Accessed 26 May 2016), 2012.
Maguire, P.J., and J.M. Woodham (eds.). *Design and Cultural Politics in Postwar Britain*. London: Leicester University Press, 1997.
Martin, R.L. *The Design of Business: Why Design Thinking is the Next Competitive Advantage*. Brighton, MA: Harvard Business Press, 2009.
Moultrie, J., P.J. Clarkson, and D. Probert. "A Tool to Evaluate Design Performance in SMEs." *International Journal of Productivity and Performance Management* 55.3/4 (2006): 184–216.
Ravi, S., and D.M. West. *Building a Design Economy in India*. New Delhi: Brookings India, 2016.
Suh, T., and I. Kwon. "Globalisation and Reluctant Buyers." *International Marketing Review* 19.6 (2002): 663–680.
Throsby, D. *Economics and Culture*. Cambridge: Cambridge University Press, 2001.
Topalian, A. "Promoting Design Leadership through Skills Development Programs." *Design Management Journal (Former Series)* 13.3 (2002): 10–18.
UNCTAD. *Creative Economy Report 2004* – United Nations Conference on Trade and Development. United Nation, 2004.
UNESCO. *Framework for Cultural Statistics*. <http://www.uis.unesco.org/culture/Pages/cinema-data-release-2011.aspx> 2009.
Velloso, J.P. d. R. O Brasil e a economia criativa: um novo mundo nos tropicos [Brazil and Creative Economy: A New World on the Tropics], (2008), Rio de Janeiro: Jose Olympio Editora. (in Portuguese)
Wikström, S. "Value Creation by Company-Consumer Interaction." *Journal of Marketing Management* 12.5 (1996): 359–374.
Wood, S. "Sustaining Crafts and Livelihoods: Handmade in India." *craft+ design enquiry* 3 (2011): 89–100.

Envisioning the future: Financialization and the Indian entertainment industry reports

Nitin Govil

ABSTRACT
It is now over 15 years since Arthur Andersen collaborated with the Federation of Indian Chambers of Commerce and Industry to issue the first 'Entertainment Industry Report,' an annual publication designed to gauge the net worth and growth potential of the Indian media industries for the global investment class. Arthur Anderson was supplanted by other transnational accounting services and management consultancies to produce the glossy trade report in association with India's largest and oldest business organization. Published in March, the report has become a key reference for journalism and cultural policy, a vehicle of industry self-promotion, and an index of the industry's corporate maturation and the overall economic health of the nation. While each report's claims on accuracy are widely accepted, this article pays close attention to the visualization of data, reading the reports as critical to an emergent financial logic that jostles uneasily with the history of trade practices in the Indian creative industries.

Like dreams, statistics are a form of wish fulfillment

– Jean Baudrillard, *Cool Memories* (147)

After a century of media industry subvention and commodification from the state and the market alike, the question remains – How can culture be counted? While creative industries policy focuses on the economic value and potential of the cultural sector, critical research traditions have claimed that what is cultural excludes that which can be counted. The tension between culture and enumeration is perhaps best expressed by Theodor Adorno, who famously insisted that 'culture is precisely that very condition that excludes a mentality that would wish to measure it' (Adorno 223).

This idea that measurement is inimical to culture runs counter to the administrative rationality of the creative industries, defined as 'the industrial components of the economy in which creativity is the input and content or intellectual property is the output' (Potts and Cunningham 233). While creative industries policy prioritizes a commercial appraisal of creative production and distribution, it is not easy to measure the economic value of talent, skill, and creativity. To be sure, technologies of quantification like copyright have emerged to map the scope and scale of the creative industries, but ongoing ethical, technological, and legal challenges attest to the continued difficulty in enumerating intangible symbolic goods and forms of cultural expression.

Unlike Western Europe and North America, where creative industries emerged as a policy imperative in the 1990s, the Global South's uneven (if not catastrophic) engagement with postindustrial transformation means that the economic potential of the creative industries has been identified only relatively recently. As the United Nations Conference on Trade and Development noted in 2004, 'creative industries already contribute to employment generation and export expansion in some leading developing countries, but at present their wider potential in unrealized' (3). However, as Stuart Cunningham notes, there is now 'growing evidence that the large developing and transitioning economies... are well aware of the significance of the creative sector's links to economic advancement' (382). In many such countries, the emerging understanding of the importance of creativity to the overall economy, beyond the older tendencies of government subsidy for the arts and the broader capitalization of cultural production, represents a distinct shift in historical relations between the state and the cultural sector.

Reflecting this shift, the creative industries have become more integral to India's projection of economic power on the global stage over the past fifteen years. This growing importance, especially in the audiovisual creative sector, can be seen as a consequence of economic liberalization beginning in the 1980s, which, along with television and home video, transformed India's relation to global audiovisual culture. The global economic expansion of the 1990s was fueled, in part, by the rise of 'emerging markets' in Brazil, Russia, India, China, and South Africa. The economic growth of these 'BRICS' nations was built on systemic transformation of the relationship between the state and the market, with formerly state-owned sectors either wholly privatized or subject to new market initiatives. World media routinely ignored the downside of economic liberalization, including significant deprivation and widespread crisis.

Terry Flew notes that, like Japan, India has been relatively late in engaging the policy implications of the creative industries (42). However, there is little doubt that like many transitional economies, India now understands its creative industries in terms of national development, with policy initiatives designed to maximize investment and export potential, increase tax revenue, strengthen educational infrastructure and short and long-term employment opportunities, and consolidate the multiplier effects of creative innovation across the economy as a whole.

In this article, I argue that India's investment in the creative sector has been mobilized by future-oriented aesthetic strategies, which I will detail below. My archive is the annual Indian entertainment industry brochure, now the standard gauge for business interest in the creative sector, produced by Indian business lobbies in collaboration with media industry confabs and international management consultancies. Since the publication of the initial Indian entertainment report in 2000 (*Strategy and Vision*), a collaboration between the Federation of Indian Chambers of Commerce and Industry (FICCI) and the now-defunct multinational accounting firm Arthur Andersen (AA), statistics measuring the overall size and growth potential of the Indian creative sector have proliferated through the press, industry, and academy. Picking up where AA left off, the Confederation of Indian Industries, the US-India Business Council, Klynveld Peat Marwick Goerdeler (KPMG), Ernst & Young, and PricewaterhouseCoopers have all released reports that are, as Kumar (26) notes, 'among the most comprehensive and exhaustive analyses of the media and entertainment industries in India.'

Launched at an industry conference themed 'Making India a Global Entertainment Superpower,' the most recent industry report lauds a multi-billion dollar industry that crosses into television, radio, print, advertising, gaming, animation, visual effects, and music industries, claiming that at the beginning of 2015, the entire media and entertainment sector was valued at well over US$16 billion, with film valued at around US$2 billion and forecasted to grow at an annual rate of 10% over the next five years (*Shooting for the Stars*).

Some cultural commentators have focused on the big numbers espoused by these reports as part of the emerging visibility of 'Brand India' and the sheer magnitude of the creative sector as integral to India's 'soft power' (Thussu 133). While there is no doubt that these reports have called attention to the growth potential of the Indian creative sector, my focus here is on the function of FICCI's collaboration with what it calls its 'knowledge partners' to produce a particular *visualization* of growth. While the graphical representation of growth and investment potential is conventional to the Western economic and analytical repertoire, its rapid adoption in the Indian creative context lays bare the crucial role of optimism in the speculative imagination (see Berlant 2011). Furthermore, the rapidity of aesthetic transformation in these reports – from simple to increasingly aggregated regimes of accuracy – is symptomatic of the compressed time-space of Asian modernity. Fabulations of futurity, these reports conscript data to a new regime designed not only to present a vision of the future but motivated by the necessity of – as the subtitle of the second AA-FICCI report put it – 'envisioning for tomorrow' (2001).

The institutional commitment to envisioning the future goes well beyond narrating a preexisting growth story. Instead, the reports are integral to the promotion of a rising 'new' India, engaging what Ravinder Kaur and Thomas Blom Hansen call 'the aesthetics of arrival.' The reports' theatrical display of statistics foregrounds 'the productive and promissory value of the spectacle in creating dream worlds for future investors – often on the basis of nothing but a promise – that also possess the capacity to turn the potential into a reality' (Kaur and Blom Hansen 5).

Figure 1, a graphical representation of aggregate creative sector growth, stages a reconciliation between facts and projection. Hard numbers may mark the limits of industry, but the

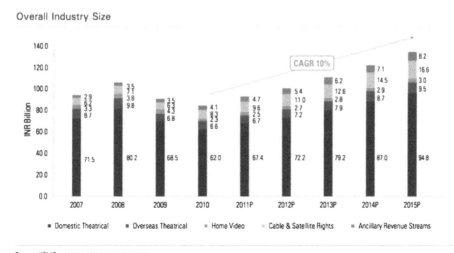

Figure 1. *Hitting the High Notes*, 2011 FICCI-KPMG entertainment industry report (61).

graphical representation of growth in the pointing arrow illustrates the desire to transcend these limits. Following this projective representational strategy, the subtitles of mid-decade entertainment industry brochures provide dreamy, tumescent figurations of possible futures: a 2005 report was subtitled *An Unfolding Opportunity*; a 2006 report, *Unraveling the Potential*; *A Growth Story Unfolds* for 2007; and by 2008, *Sustaining Growth*. 2009's report, *In the Interval, but Ready for the Next Act*, sustained the theme of arousal in similarly vigorous fashion. This performance of excitation is linguistically related to the entrepreneurial, which, as Miranda Joseph reminds us, is 'one who "gets up" entertainments' (494).

In this article, I attempt to come to terms with such accounts of 'rising' India, which means not only investigating the discourse on India's emergence, but also critiquing the forms of imaging and imagining through which this emergence has been represented. I locate the role of the entertainment industry reports within a transforming political economy of media as management consultancies have pushed the Indian creative sector from national to global relevance over the past fifteen years. I also argue that the preponderance of statistics in these entertainment industry reports has helped to resolve the creative industries' perceived deficit of reflexivity. If numbers serve 'as the currency of policy' (Hartley et al. 156), then the graphical representation of industry data makes the argument for enshrining the creative sector among other monuments of Indian growth. Critical to redressing the sense of inferiority within the film sector in particular, numbers are the very evidence of industry itself – proof of its industriousness. In other words, numbers do not only supply sociotechnical evidence of Indian economic change. Rather, enumeration itself has become a signifier of transformation within the Indian creative industries. My purpose is to think through the genres of data visualization designed to quantify creative growth in graphical form, but also to examine the 'epistemic cultures' (Knorr-Cetina 1999) that nurture and define a particular aesthetic form of enumerative reasoning within the creative sector.

Enumeration, from the national to the global

March 2000 saw the release of AA's industry report *Strategy and Vision*, drafted in collaboration with FICCI, an organization founded in 1927 to articulate the interest of Indian capitalists to the nationalist struggle for independence. Beholden to an economic nationalism, FICCI was charged with opening domestic industry to more Indian management and encouraging entrepreneurship and autonomy for Indian manufacturing and banking. By the end of the twentieth century, however, FICCI was reconciled to a more global outlook. Reflecting the state and market mandate on foreign investment, FICCI employed the services of the Chicago-based AA to enumerate the size and scale of the Indian film industry. The ensuing industry report emphasized bringing the media industry in line with the information technology sector through accounting transparency and the corporatization of a notoriously complicated entertainment sector.

During fieldwork in Delhi and Bombay in late 2000, I heard a lot about this slim but glossy FICCI-AA report. Many journalists had a shorter executive summary version, but few possessed the full report. Priced at Rs.10,000 (then over US$ 225), the report was clearly designed for elite circulation among the policy and entertainment sector and was not widely disseminated to reporters and academics. In terms of my own access, it was only when I met a senior official at the Ministry of Information and Broadcasting that I even saw a physical copy of the report. During a conversation about Indian film's intensifying connections with

Hollywood, the official called for an aide to escort me to a storage room, where the aqua blue reports were stacked like the building blocks of some future architectural structure. Back in the main office, with my talismanic copy of the report in hand, the official said that he would be grateful if I publicized its findings when I got back to the U.S. I consider this article to be a somewhat belated payment of that debt.

In any event, the price of the report was not to offset the cost of research since it merely repackaged a number of widely available Film Federation of India statistics. Those in the industry also knew that AA had done the consulting work for free in the hopes for future Indian entertainment partnerships down the line. Instead, the price-point was in line with management consulting studies, familiar to the business community since the entry of the global consulting firms in India in the late 1980s. At that time, the American multinational management consulting firm McKinsey was hired for a turnaround project at Hindustan Motors. South Asians in positions of prominence at the firm, including Rajat Gupta, then head of McKinsey's Chicago office, subsequently visited India in 1988 and began the process of setting up an India office in the early 1990s. Consulting firms like McKinsey and others advocated for widespread corporate restructuring in India, changing Indian business culture and encouraging institutional transformation towards efficiency and performance. These firms were integral to the perception of India in the global investment community and encouraged the entry of a host of multinational professional networks providing business support from tax and accounting services to management consulting, portfolio analysis, and business process improvement.

The creative industry's interest in tax and auditing support marked a shift from the consultancy strategy, but was nevertheless part of a trend in the multinational enumeration of the Indian audiovisual sector. Three such network firms have been prominent in providing auditing support for the creative industry, especially KPMG (with global offices in the Netherlands), Ernst & Young (headquartered in the UK), and PricewaterhouseCoopers (also headquartered in the UK). However, it was the 2000 AA report that framed the blueprint for what Aswin Punathembekar argues has become 'the new modes of speculation demanded by new sources of capital' (69). Given the casual labor endemic in the Indian creative sector, the report was less focused on employment statistics than other national analyses. Instead, it focused on projected turnover, exports, and tax revenues for the creative sectors. The report considered tax revenues for the government, revenue projections of each sector, and household penetration of various media technologies. The industry potential of Indian filmed entertainment was measured in terms of increased regional demand, export potential, and the projection of India as a base for animated and feature film production.

Taken as a whole, the 2000 FICCI-AA report is, essentially, a call for increased government recognition of the economic potential of the Indian creative sector. However, over the fifteen-year history of these FICCI reports, the emphasis has shifted gradually from the national to the global. The 2000 report insists throughout that the government respond more definitively to creative sector challenges. Each section of the report ends with a 'What's in it for the Government' statement, detailing spectrum leasing possibilities, direct and indirect employment opportunities, raising foreign exchange earnings, and benefits to ancillary industries. The key interests of the creative industries are summarized in terms of demands from the state: rationalization of tax rates across the country; continued central government recognition for the film industry; anti-piracy at the municipal level coordinated to international intellectual property harmonization; stable licensing schemes for broadcast licenses; privatization of a government-controlled television network; changing the function of the censor board; changing banking and financial policies; and simplifying regulation.

Consolidating a fifteen-year shifting from the national to the global, the 2015 FICCI-KPMG report begins with an acknowledgment of the current government's 'optimistic outlook' and makes bold claims on the growth potential of the industry. From the smaller and more modest sectorial projections of the earlier iterations of the report, which consider the growth potential of each area of the creative industries separately and are primarily tasked with illustrating broad trends in graphic color (Figures 2(a) and (b)), the 2015 report is focused on precision and aggregation (Figure 3).

Furthermore, unlike the 2000 report's national focus, the 2015 report positions India strategically within a transforming global economy:

> Offering the world's largest base of a young workforce, an expanding middle-class constituting one of the biggest consumer markets and a robust, well-functioning democratic system, India, along with its pro-reforms government, is now scripting a turnaround story. The global economy is struggling to gain momentum, as China suffers a slowdown, the euro-zone slips into deflation, and Japan's economy is too soft to absorb the fiscal consolidation plan. Despite the shaky global economy, India is performing relatively well, with a stable macroeconomic environment (inflation eased while the current account deficit came under control, bolstering the economic outlook). The Indian economy is on a strong footing, with FY15 growth estimated at 7.4 per cent while FY16 growth was pegged at 8 to 8.5 per cent. As a result, there is a marked shift in investor sentiment towards India: global investors increasingly see India with renewed interest and optimism, thanks to an optimistic government at the centre and its reform agenda. The government's recent budget announcements underpinned the sentiment further. Improved business sentiment together with policy reforms could boost the country's long-term growth potential. This growth story extends itself across Media and Entertainment sectors. We estimate that the Indian market is poised to grow at a CAGR of 13.9 per cent, to grow from INR1026 billion in 2014 to reach INR1964 billion by 2019, a growth rate that is almost double that of the global media and entertainment industry (*Shooting* 2).

Situating the creative industries within wider macroeconomic growth suggests that by 2015, the argument about creative industry contribution to the economic health of state seems to have been largely settled. The presence of the unelaborated acronym CAGR – for compound annual growth rate – suggests that the focus is on futurity and speculation rather than an argument for how to rectify a present crisis.

This was hardly the case just fifteen years ago, as the creative sector vied for greater government appreciation. In the 2000 FICCI-AA report, the opening statement from FICCI President G.P. Goenka notes that, 'in India, the entertainment industry has largely progressed without much of [sic] government incentive and support. The very fact that the business of entertainment has now come to occupy center stage is a pointer to its tremendous untapped potential' (v). Goenka's sentiment tapped into the prevailing wisdom at the turn of the century. At the National Conference on 'Challenges Before Indian Media,' the May 1998 event organized by FICCI and the Film Federation of India that served as the template for the annual FICCI-FRAMES confabs in the years to come, many speakers spoke bitterly about the lack of government support for the film industry in particular. Speaking at the conference on the eve of India's nuclear test at Pokhran in the Rajasthani Thar Desert, FICCI's President K.K. Modi enjoined the industry to the patriotic cause:

SOUTH ASIAN CREATIVE AND CULTURAL INDUSTRIES

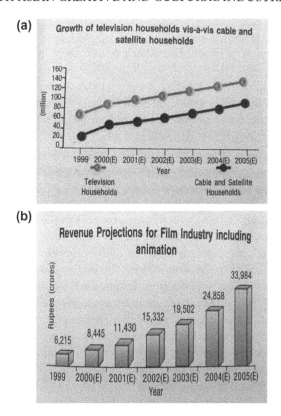

Figure 2. *Strategy and Vision*, 2000 FICCI-AA entertainment industry report (15, 29).

The Indian media and entertainment industry: size and projections

Overall industry size (INR billion) (For Calendar Years)	2008	2009	2010	2011	2012	2013	2014	Growth in 2014 over 2013	2015P	2016P	2017P	2018P	2019P	CAGR (2014-2019P)
TV	241.0	257.0	297.0	329.0	370.1	417.2	474.9	13.8%	543.2	631.2	739.6	854.6	975.5	15.5%
Print	172.0	175.2	192.9	208.8	224.1	243.1	263.4	8.3%	284.5	307.1	331.9	358.0	386.8	8.0%
Films	104.4	89.3	83.3	92.9	112.4	125.3	126.4	0.9%	136.3	155.6	170.7	186.3	204.0	10.0%
Radio	8.4	8.3	10.0	11.5	12.7	14.6	17.2	17.6%	19.6	22.3	27.0	32.7	39.5	18.1%
Music	7.4	7.8	8.6	9.0	10.6	9.6	9.8	2.3%	10.4	12.0	14.2	16.9	18.9	14.0%
OOH	16.1	13.7	16.5	17.8	18.2	19.3	22.0	14.0%	24.4	27.1	29.6	32.2	35.1	9.8%
Animation and VFX	17.5	20.1	23.7	31.0	35.3	39.7	44.9	13.1%	51.0	58.7	68.5	80.6	95.5	16.3%
Gaming	7.0	8.0	10.0	13.0	15.3	19.2	23.5	22.4%	27.5	31.8	35.4	40.0	45.8	14.3%
Digital Advertising	6.0	8.0	10.0	15.4	21.7	30.1	43.5	44.5%	62.5	84.0	115.3	138.2	162.5	30.2%
Total	580	587	652	728	821	918	1,026	11.7%	1159	1330	1532	1740	1964	13.9%

Source: KPMG in India analysis

Figure 3. *Shooting for the Stars*, 2015 FICCI-KPMG entertainment industry report (9).

Whenever there has been a crisis, this industry has come forward and supported the nation. Be it war with Pakistan, or in times of great national tragedy, we have seen that people from this sector have come forward and given all help to the nation. In spite of that, if we find that this industry has not been supported by the nation, there is something radically wrong somewhere (1998).

At an earlier panel at the same conference, Amit Khanna was more succinct in his indictment, claiming that 'successive governments have done precious little for this business and if the Industry has survived for so many decades it is not with [the] Government's help but in spite of it' (1998). Industry recognition for the film sector was finally announced at the end of the conference, testifying to the importance of the national as an index of creative production and distribution. Sanctioned by state and market bureaucracies, creative industries are implicated in the processes of national legitimation in the domain of law (through intellectual property, authorship and domicile), propriety in the routines of cultural work (through labor laws and censorship), and exclusivity in the field of cultural policy (through quotas, import restrictions, spectrum allocation and communications infrastructures).

Historically, the relationship between cinema and indigenous development was undermined by relatively marginal support from Indian state and market institutions. After Independence in 1947, the Indian state's commitment to rapid modernization focused on nationalizing banking, transportation, postal, telecommunication and electronic sectors (McDowell 1997). Cinema was not included among the key projects of Indian developmental modernity. Cinema did serve, however, as a vehicle for social reformers who understood it as indecent, akin to gambling and prostitution, in need of regulation through taxation and censorship (Prasad 1998). Beginning in the 1950s, the alignment between the regulation of screen consumption and the management of civic virtue underscored the creation of import/export councils, development corporations, and enquiry committees that allowed the state to function as both 'patron and disciplinarian' for the Indian film industries (Pendakur 59).

During this national transition, Hollywood served a critical role in marshaling arguments for greater Indian film industry subsidy (see Govil 2015). These arguments relied on Hollywood's centrality to American economic power and insisted on following a similar model in India. For example, a 1939 pamphlet called the *Place of Film in National Planning*, written by K.S. Hirlekar, a key figure in the early institutional organization of Indian film industries, argues that film 'is playing an important role in the progress of all advanced nations of the world,' and that the neglect of cinema by central and provincial Indian governments demonstrates that they have 'not fully realized the tremendous latent power ... of film in educating the masses, especially the illiterates, for individual and national advancement' (1, 9). A few years later, as secretary to an Indian delegation on a study tour of American and British studios in 1945, Hirlekar noted the importance of the film industries to domestic economies, claiming that 'it is urgently necessary that an organized and centralized effort must be made to put the film industry in this country ... on an stable and progressive foundation' and that 'it is the State, and the State alone which can take the lead in supplying the finance for its organized and well-thought-out development' (Report of the Indian Film Industry's Mission to Europe & America, 59). Hirlekar's words echo the history of statistical inquiry, which claimed the national as the enumerating center for the aggregation of data.

Furthermore, Hirlekar's location of the institutional and statistical imperative with the state apparatus echoes a longstanding critique of underdeveloped enumeration within the

Indian film sector. 'The industry itself is in such a muddle that the initiated and the uninitiated hardly know which way to turn: and if the industry is in a muddle progress is positively impossible,' wrote Niranjan Pal in *Filmland* in 1931. Since that time, Indian cinema has been routinely criticized for its inability to accurately enumerate its activities. This deficit of industrial reflexivity was raised at a 1935 Indian film conference, where M. Visvesvaraya noted the 'principal wants of the industry':

> The great need of the industry is reliable statistics, which is the yardstick by which every industry is measured. To get a correct idea of its condition, one must know such facts, as the number of cinema theatres, the number of producing establishments, capital invested, value of machinery and raw materials used, profits earned, number employed in the industry, wages paid, the number of persons attending the theatres in a week, and similar particulars. Reliable information under many of these heads is wanting at present (4).

Such frank assessments of the unreliability of numbers permeate the history of Indian film discourse, where the industry is presented as a statistical enigma, an improvisational enterprise driven by dubious numbers.

Less than impressive numbers supported even those policy frameworks that called for more stringent enumeration. The Indian Cinematographic Committee received 320 responses from over 4300 questionnaires sent out in preparation for its 1927 report, which formed the basis of our understanding of India production and distribution in the silent era. In its 1951 report, compiled from the circulation of 7140 questionnaires of which 463 were returned (Jain 9), the Film Enquiry Committee claimed that the 'figures given ... to illustrate the progress attained by the industry are not comprehensive nor can their accuracy be fully vouched for. That cannot be so in the very nature of things' (Report of the Film Enquiry Committee, 14). The 1969 Report of the Enquiry Committee on Film Censorship sent out 14,000 questionnaires of which 900 responses were received.

Of course, the Indian film industries have long rehearsed ways to account for themselves through formal and informal inquiry. In the nineteen-teens, municipal governments concerned about the fire hazards of makeshift theaters compiled lists of permanent and itinerant cinemas. Censorship regimes counted films in the process of certifying them. Foreign distribution outfits and local entrepreneurs kept records of imported exposed stock for duty purposes. Photography studios and practitioners monitored the trade in new and used film equipment. Box-office takes were tallied and entertainment taxes were levied. Film clubs and societies polled their members to get a sense of audience preferences. These varied practices produced disparate sets of figures tabulated by various state and municipal authorities and industry associations, but only occasionally combined in an aggregate sense of 'an industry.'

As Tejaswini Ganti (2015) has argued somewhat counter-intuitively, the ambiguity of data collection practices particularly in the Bombay film industry has actually stabilized historical relations between production, distribution, and exhibition by creating common frames of reference between them. Not only does each sector claim, create, and dispute box-office returns, but the battle over numerical accuracy helps gird their self-understanding as mutually antagonistic sectors, each attached to its own regimes of reputational anxiety.

Ganti's assertion that ambiguity is constitutive, generative, and productive focuses on the uncertain status and accuracy of box-office returns in the film industry. However, what she characterizes as a poverty of information seems to have been replaced by the proliferation of data not so much regarding box-office revenue, but pertaining to the size and growth potential of the media industries as a *whole*. In fact, since the early 2000s, globalization has reversed the marginality of accuracy and aggregation. The collection of data, the production of statistics, and the graphical representation of aggregate trends helped to render the creative industries legible within global financial dynamics. Furthermore, these reports legitimized the management consultancy as the long sought-after central agency charged with measurement, initiating a movement towards visualization practices that would recursively define both the form and content of enumeration.

The visualization of the financial fact

As I have argued, the first FICCI-Arthur Andersen report signaled an empirical turn in the measurement of Indian creative production and distribution. In this sense, the report was the opening salvo in the battle over enumeration. Addressing the creative sector's long-standing lament over statistical rigor, the numerical and graphical expression of cultural value in subsequent entertainment industry reports served as an acknowledgment of the virtues of quantification. By yoking analytical tools to narrative genres of promotion, these reports helped create the framework for the emergence of enumeration as the dominant mode of inscription in the creative industries. In this logic, numbers serve as both a metric of comparison and a mode of conversion from industry to economy.

It's not surprising that the close affinities of purpose between auditing and investment agencies – despite laws mandating their separation – have inaugurated an enumerative regime charged with maximizing optimism about the upward momentum of the Indian creative sector. The creative industry's investment in such calculating logics is inseparable from the visualization of data. The fact-minded creative sector's shift towards the graphical display of statistical information has engaged a palette of visualization techniques designed to represent the distribution of data and the creation of numerical and proportional comparisons including bar charts, 2D and 3D pie charts, line graphs, and occasional histograms. Designed to represent upward momentum with an elegant simplicity, the reports link visual presentation and maximal optimism. Graphical simplicity implies a resonance between enumeration and objectivity, creating the impression that the data is an indexical representation of the 'real' industry. Whereas enumeration was something of an interpretive art in previous statistical efforts, the reports' embrace of a graphical visuality is commensurate with the creative industry's desire for transparency.

In 'Size Matters' (Govil 2010), I described the new accounting culture of the Indian film industries as distinctive from the older 'fuzzier' forms of calculation. Here, I borrowed the term 'fuzzy' from Sudipta Kaviraj's usage, which he deploys to describe the vague boundaries of traditional community in India prior to their enumeration by colonial British authority. Following Kaviraj's usage, fuzziness does not imply imprecision or social practices outside rational and affective understanding (56). Instead, a 'fuzzy' sense of quantification in the historical forms of accounting would be relatively indeterminate, motivated by practical considerations of immediate and tactical alignment, combination, and assessment rather than aggregation oriented to some future purpose. In the past 15 years, there has been a gradual, but marked trend towards representational strategies geared towards greater accuracy as the creative industries shifted their own account of themselves. In this sense, visualization regimes (Figure 4) tie legitimation to legibility. It is not that the data or its representation is inherently deceptive or lacks fidelity; rather that the graphics simplify the business of counting culture in a manner that, following Edward Tufte's critique of

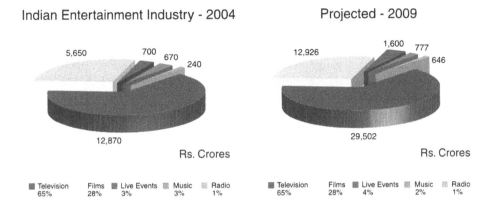

Figure 4. *An Unfolding Opportunity*, FICCI-PWC 2005 entertainment industry report, Executive Summary (12).

Microsoft Powerpoint presentations, 'turns information into a sales pitch' (Tufte 4). This impoverishment attests to the social role of enumeration as management consultancies have subsumed the traditional advocacy roles taken on by government ministries, state and municipal cultural councils and industry lobbies. The appeal of simplification is designed, as Wendy Espeland notes, to 'produce public, authoritative knowledge that makes them appear legible to outsiders' (56).

While the genres of data visualization in the entertainment industry reports are the result of recently implemented managerial cultures, they are also part of much longer historical trends. Data visualization is part of an array of epistemological strategies for regularizing abstraction, part of a modern imperative to connect, share, and translate knowledge across scientific inquiry, expedition, exploration, and imperial expansion. Such strategies for unification, combination, and comparison across institutional variation take place within what Bruno Latour calls 'centers of calculation,' where data is recorded, combined, and accumulated in a way that 'facilitates the proliferation of enumerative enquiry across networks of practice' (304). The proliferating function of visualization also aligns with the modern political relationship between measurement and governmentality, a framework that institutionalized an audit culture whose 'calculative practices typify modern society' (Rottenburg et al. 20).

As the chart indicates (Figure 4), the graphical practices of the Indian entertainment industry reports regularize and translate difference between creative sectors in monetary terms, allowing for stable aggregation within a circular whole. Glossy both in their materiality and superficiality, these visualization strategies have contributed to the ubiquitously bland deployment of numbers as euphemism, the 'business of bigness' that facilitates the recognition of Indian creative industries with the global political economy.

While these visualization practices are the legacy of modern inscriptive practices, they can also change rapidly over a short period of time. The emergence of the management consultancy and international auditing firm as an enumerating agency in India – one that both does and represents the counting – resulted in an uneven visual regime as the entertainment industry reports settled on representational styles that could be durable over time. The flurry of reports during the first decade of consultancy and auditing enumeration saw a few failed experiments in graphical excess, like the absurd chart (Figure 5), which is both hard to read and requires multiple confirmations of the relative costs of film production: the relative size of each colored bar; the percentage terms above each bar; and the corresponding percentage on the vertical gauge on the left-hand side. Eschewing a simple single bar or a pie-chart, PWC chose an unnecessarily complicated representation as if beholden to a *sui generis* graphical imperative.

When there was continuity across annual entertainment industry reports, minor variations and corrections could still be made. For example, in 2006 (see Figure 6), the pie charts of 2005 (Figure 4) are retained, with creative sectors represented as segments and the obviousness of aggregation still suggesting an entertainment industry whole. However, the 2006 report shifts the visual logic away from monetary comparison towards a proportional comparison, with the relationship between industries demonstrated in relative sizes and confirmed by percentages. In the space of one year, the design philosophy has shifted, while national aggregation remains confirmed.

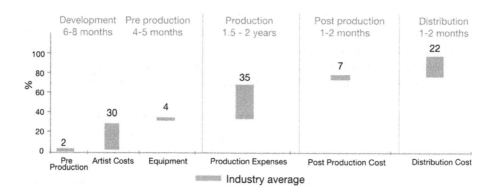

Figure 5. *Indian Entertainment and Media Outlook* 2010 (56). Source: PwC analysis.

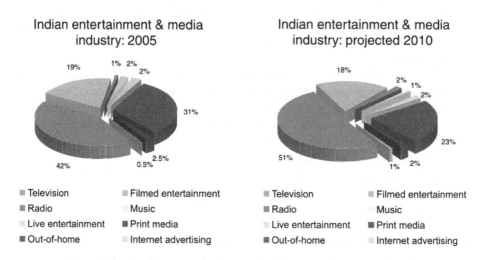

Figure 6. *Unraveling the Potential*, FICCI-PWC 2006 industry report, Executive Summary (14).

The following year, data visualization was more comprehensively revised. Issued in the aftermath of a record annual high mark in foreign investment flows in the Indian creative sector, the 2007 report paid special attention to the possibilities of convergent media production and distribution across platforms and the importance of accurate audience measurement. The representation of aggregation shifted dramatically from previous years, with a focus not so much on the relative sizes of each creative sector, but a consideration of their growth potential going forward for 6 years and annualized into a CAGR, or combined annual growth rate, a key metric for investment purposes (Figure 7).

In early 2007, buoyed by the previous years highpoint, the world entertainment press was fixated on foreign investment in the Indian creative sector. In its coverage of the March 2007 FICCI-Frames industry conference, the American trade journal *Variety* noted that 'India's movie business is suddenly legitimate – and awash in cash' (Frater A1). Citing the availability of corporate and Hollywood funding, initial public offerings of film-related businesses on the Bombay stock exchange, and international venture capital interest in film sector, *Variety* insisted that the Indian film business was no longer an 'impenetrable enigma for Western firms.'

Marked by a new numerical precision, new aesthetic conventions like this chart (Figure 7) were launched in the spirit of a new legibility. On the PWC website, the executive summary of the 2007 report was issued with a somewhat strange note documenting the process:

> The report has been prepared on the basis of information obtained from key industry players, trade associations, government agencies, trade publications, and other industry sources. The performance trends in different segments of the industry were analyzed and an attempt was made to identify the underlying factors. Models were developed to quantify the impact of each of these factors, to create a forecast scenario. PWC's professional expertise, institutional knowledge and global resources of knowledge and excellence were applied to review and adjust those values wherever required. The entire process was then examined for internal consistency and transparency vis-a-vis prevailing industry wisdom. Feedback from key industry players was subjected to a rigorous validation process to ensure that it was consistent and conformed to the industry feel (Notes to the Editor 2009).

The notion of an 'industry feel' corresponded to an earlier affective alignment between sense and corporatism. At the film industry recognition event in 1998, industry leader Amit Khanna (1998) noted that 'corporatization is an attitude,' inadvertently locating industry performance

	2004	2005	2006E	2007F	2008F	2009F	2010F	2011F	CAGR
Television	128,700	158,500	191,200	219,900	266,000	331,300	431,000	519,000	22%
Print Media	87,800	109,500	127,900	144,000	162,200	182,300	206,500	232,000	13%
Filmed Entertainment	59,900	68,100	84,500	96,800	112,000	126,450	146,000	175,000	16%
Radio	2,400	3,200	5,000	6,500	8,500	11,000	14,000	17,000	28%
Music	6,700	7,000	7,200	7,400	7,500	7,600	8,000	8,700	4%
OOH advertising	8,500	9,000	10,000	12,500	14,500	16,500	19,000	21,500	17%
Live Entertainment	7,000	8,000	9,000	11,000	13,000	16,000	18,000	19,000	16%
Internet advertising	600	1,000	1,600	2,700	4,200	6,000	8,200	9,500	43%
Total*	311,600	364,300	436,500	500,800	588,300	697,150	850,700	1,001,700	18%

Figure 7. *A Growth Story Unfolds*, FICCI-PWC 2007 industry report (24).

within a performance of deferral and corporatization initiatives within the 'not-yet' of capital (Chakrabarty). Similarly, the idea of 'industry feel' in the 2007 report was framed within the new speculative logic of CAGR, a distinctive numerological figure orienting the creative industries towards the future. Of course, in a reversal from previous decades, the consulting community had become much more committed to outcomes rather than ideas (Mahanta 2013). In addition, the creative industry's obsession with statistics and foreign investment inculcated a projection of growth as a way to consolidate claims on the future. The representation of CAGR is a kind of aesthetics of deferred arrival, visualized as an asymptotic journey where the upward arrow of progress never arrives at its destination, let alone a plateau.

At times in these reports, the representation of growth becomes remarkably unmoored from an indexical consideration of the 'real' industry or from the speculative projection of compounded profitability, floating freely as abstract representations of potential. For example, in the following figures, sound echoes the growth story of innumerable bar graphs (Figure 8) and money stacks itself in strikingly familiar graphical precision (Figure 9).

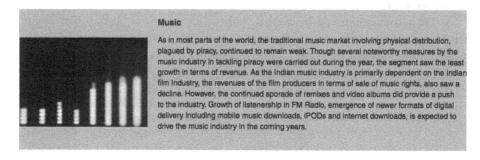

Figure 8. *An Unfolding Opportunity*, FICCI-PWC industry report 2005, Executive Summary (10).

Figure 9. *In the Interval, but Ready for the Next Act*, FICCI-KPMG 2009 Report (20).

Such abstractions stage the collapse of the distinction between the real and imagined economy, a breakdown that is key to the logic of financialization (see Martin 2013). Perhaps more than any prior graphical representation of economic data, these abstractions speak to the creative industry's new imperatives of sense-making in the projective register. How else can these optimisms be captured but through such forms of spectacle? As the history of the entertainment reports suggests, what was once quite reflexively described as an artful and naggingly incoherent practice has distilled into a quantifiable culture. Yet, as the portraits of growth above demonstrate, the transition from impressionism to utility can only be figured in aesthetic terms that paint a picture of the future that even enumeration cannot fully signify. Despite the renunciation of previous enumerative strategies, the forms that direct such aesthetics of advancement demonstrate that the passage from the gnomic to the statistical is anything but straightforward.

Disclosure statement

No potential conflict of interest was reported by the author.

References

Adorno, Theodor. "Scientific Experiences of a European Scholar in America." *Critical Models: Interventions and Catchwords*. Trans. Henry W. Pickford. New York: Columbia University Press, 2005. 215–44.
Baudrillard, Jean. *Cool Memories*. Trans. Chris Turner. New York: Verso, 1990.
Berlant, Lauren. *Cruel Optimism*. Durham: Duke University Press, 2011.
Chakrabarty, Dipesh. *Provincializing Europe: Post-Colonial Thought and Historical Difference*. Delhi: Oxford University Press, 2000, 47–71.
"Creative Industries and Development." United Nations Conference on Trade and Development, São Paulo, 13–18 June 2004. Document TD(XI)/BP/13, released 4 June, 2004.
Cunningham, Stuart. "Trojan Horse or Rorschach Blot: Creative Industries Discourse Around the World." *International Journal of Cultural Policy* 15.4 (2009): 375–86.
Envisioning for Tomorrow: Indian Entertainment Industry Report 2001. Mumbai: FICCI/AA, 2001.
Espeland, Wendy. "Narrating Numbers." *The World of Indicators: The Making of Governmental Knowledge through Quantification*. Eds. Rottenburg, Richard, et al. Cambridge: Cambridge University Press, 2015, 56–75.
Flew, Terry. *The Creative Industries: Culture and Policy*. Thousand Oaks, CA: Sage, 2012.
Frater, Patrick. "Strike Up the Bank." *Variety* 19 Mar. 2007.
Ganti, Tejaswini. "Fuzzy Numbers: The Productive Nature of Ambiguity in the Hindi Film Industry." *Comparative Studies of South Asia, Africa, and the Middle East* 35.3 (2015): 451–65.
Govil, Nitin. *Orienting Hollywood: A Century of Film Culture Between Los Angeles and Bombay*. New York: New York University Press, 2015.
Govil, Nitin. "Size Matters." *BioScope: South Asian Screen Studies* 1.2 (2010): 105–109.
A Growth Story Unfolds: The Indian Entertainment and Media Industry. Delhi: FICCI/PWC, 2007.
Hartley, John, et al. *Key Concepts in Creative Industries*. Thousand Oaks, CA: Sage, 2013.
Hirlekar, K.S.. *Place of Film in National Planning*. Bombay: Visual Education Society, 1939.

Hitting the High Notes: FICCI-KPMG Indian Media and Entertainment Industry Report 2011. Delhi: FICCI/KPMG, 2011.
Indian Entertainment and Media Outlook 2010. Delhi: FICCI/PWC, 2010.
In the Interval, but Ready for the Next Act: FICCI-KPMG Media & Entertainment Industry Report. Delhi: FICCI/KPMG, 2009.
Jain, Rikhab Dass. *The Economic Aspects of the Film Industry in India*. Delhi: Atma Ram & Sons, 1960.
Joseph, Miranda. "Investing in the Cruel Entrepreneurial University." *South Atlantic Quarterly* 114.3 (July 2015): 491–511.
Khanna, Amit. "Industry Status for the Film Industry." Presentation at the National Conference on "Challenges Before Indian Cinema", May 10, Mumbai, 1998.
Kaur, Ravinder, and Thomas Blom Hansen. "Aesthetics of Arrival: Spectacle, Capital, Novelty in Post-Reform India." *Identities: Global Studies in Culture and Power* 23.3 (2015): 265-275.
Kaviraj, Sudipta. *The Imaginary Institution of India: Politics and Ideas*. New York: Columbia University Press, 2010.
Knorr-Cetina, Karin. *Epistemic Cultures: How the Sciences Make Knowledge*. Cambridge: Harvard University Press, 1999.
Kumar, Shanti. "Media Industries in India: An Emerging Regional Framework." *Media Industries Journal* 1.2 (2015). Web. 1 Nov. 2015. <www.mediaindustriesjournal.org>.
Latour, Bruno. *Pandora's Hope*. Cambridge: Harvard University Press, 1991.
Mahanta, Vinod. "How are McKinsey, BCC, Bain, AT Kearney and the Likes Playing the Game in India?" *The Economic Times* 2 Apr. 2013. Web. 5 Nov. 2015.
Martin, Randy. "After Economy? Social Logics of the Derivative." *Social Text* 31 (2013): 83–106.
McDowell, Stephen. *Globalization, Liberalization and Policy Change*. London: MacMillan, 1997.
Modi, K.K. Valedictory Address at the National Conference on "Challenges Before Indian Cinema", May 10, Mumbai, 1998.
"Notes to the Editor: About the Indian Entertainment and Media Industry – A Growth Story Unfolds." Web. 23 May 2009. <www.pwc.com>
Pal, Niranjan. "India and the Film Industry I." *Filmland*, 9 May 1931.
Pendakur, Manjunath. *Indian Popular Cinema: Industry, Ideology, and Consciousness*. Cresskill: Hampton Press, 2003.
Potts, Jason, and Stuart Cunningham. "Four Models of the Creative Industries." *International Journal of Cultural Policy* 14.3 (2008): 233–247.
Prasad, Madhava. *Wages of Freedom: Fifty Years of the Indian Nation-State*. Ed. Partha Chatterjee. New Delhi: Oxford University Press, 1998.
Punathambekar, Aswin. *From Bombay to Bollywood: The Making of a Global Media Industry*. New York: New York University Press, 2013.
Report of the Film Enquiry Committee. New Delhi: Government of India Press, 1951.
Report of the Indian Film Industry's Mission to Europe & America. Bombay: Avanti Prakashan, 1946.
Rottenburg, Richard, et al., eds. *The World of Indicators: The Making of Governmental Knowledge through Quantification*. Cambridge: Cambridge University Press, 2015.
Shooting for the Stars: FICCI/KPMG Indian Media and Entertainment Industry Report 2015. Delhi: FICCI/KPMG, 2015.
Strategy and Vision: Indian Entertainment Industry Report 2000. Mumbai: FICCI/AA, 2000.
Thussu, Daya. *Communicating India's Soft Power: Buddha to Bollywood*. New York: Palgrave MacMillan, 2013.
Tufte, Edward. *The Cognitive Style of PowerPoint: Pitching Out Corrupts Within*. Cheshire, CT: Graphics Press, 2001.
An Unfolding Opportunity: The Indian Entertainment Industry. Delhi: FICCI/PWC, 2005.
Unraveling the Potential: The Indian Entertainment and Media Industry. Delhi: FICCI/PWC, 2006.
Visvesvaraya, M. *Present Position of the Motion Picture Industry*. Bombay: Times of India Press, 1935.

Bahrisons New Delhi: Commerce and creativity in Khan Market

Emma Varughese

In the early 1950s, Khan Market in New Delhi was starting to establish itself and shop spaces were being allocated to refugees from the North West Frontier Province (NWFP). One refugee took up a shop at great expense in order to set up a bookstore which has come to be known as 'Bahrisons'. Khan Market these days is an upmarket district of New Delhi where the well-to-do sip tea, shop and browse the latest books. Needless to say that Bahrisons' continuing success relies on the creative industries of domestic India, a sector that has witnessed and undergone immense change, particularly post millennium. Although the premises have not changed greatly from the early days – the floor to ceiling books and narrow aisles – the manner in which books are selected, sold and marketed takes place against the backdrop of New India. This interview explores these changes in some detail and is framed by discussion of location (Khan Market), commerce and marketing strategies

Bahrisons in 2016, a view from the pavement. Image © Bahrisons, A. Malhotra.

and post-millennial India. The interview is conducted with Bahrisons CEO, Anuj Bahri who also runs Red Ink Literary Agency; an extension of the Bahrisons book business. The interview explores issues of: commerce in Khan Market, impact of economic liberalisation, author representation, the explosion of popular fiction post-2000 and marketing of books.

[EDV] Anuj Bahri, Khan Market these days is known as an up-market sector of New Delhi, has this always been the case? How would you describe the area around the original shop (that is now Bahrisons) and could you say a little about how and when the unit was purchased?

[AB] Khan Market from its inception always had an up-market customer base. In the earlier days of the market from the 1950s till the later part of the 1970s, Khan Market was a lazy 'mom n pop stores' sort of a market. The main trade of the market was daily groceries, fruit and vegetables, chemists, cloth material stores and tailors – with the exception of bookstores. Somehow the market was always visited by the upper crust alongside a very international mix of customers. Diplomats considered this a good place to meet and shop in peace without people disturbing them. The market in essence of size and international appeal has not changed much, but the basic character has changed drastically. From the small independently owned shops, there are more branded stores seen in the market.

The shop Bahrisons was purchased in bits and parts. One part was purchased in the initial days when the store was started and the other two were slowly converted from rentals to ownership – as and when the pocket would allow.

The shop started in the central part of the plot with a small collection of stationery and comics. Slowly the shop grew and the collection increased from just comics to

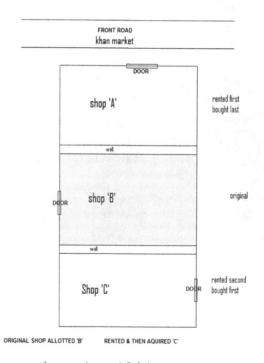

The floor plan of Bahrisons over the years. Image © Bahrisons.

novels and popular books and finally on to non-fiction. The walls had to be removed one by one to give the shop more space and an airy look and then there was the change from rented to ownership. It was always a step at a time, but I believe, always a step in the right direction.

[EDV] Every time I enter Bahrisons, there is a sense of wonder as my eyes scan the books stacked floor to ceiling. This visual, of the books reaching from floor to ceiling is a hallmark of the place for me as is the experience of browsing whilst others brush or push past and the presence of ladders and steps standing to attention against the various shelves. Has the shop, in its book selling avatar always been arranged this way? What are people's reactions to the manner in which the shop is stocked and books are displayed? How does your staff interact with customers – browsing and seeking particular items?

[AB] A book shop by nature should be chaotic. There is a certain amount of fun in rummaging through all the hundreds of books to find the gem that you are looking for. A good reader enjoys spending time in a bookshop, so why cut short his visit for a quick 'buy and run'. A good reader will enjoy searching through the stacks of books – there are no complaints there. The fun of searching for what you want is different from picking up the first new book on the shelf. The staff is there to help (if you ask) and they love the idea of customers searching for their own books and browsing through the store.

[EDV] Are you not concerned that this approach to 'selling' may mean that you miss out on book sales? It seems that your strategy of selling on the shop floor at Bahrisons is quite different from the more aggressive forms of marketing and selling we see in urban centres today.

[AB] There is no strategy to bookselling in my opinion – either you have a good collection or a basic collection. People do get aggressive about selling books, but you as a reader are only interested in a good collection. So no matter how aggressive the bookseller wants to be, if your collection cannot speak for itself or the intellect of the curator, there will be no sales at all.

The floor-to-ceiling book shelves at Bahrisons. Image © Bahrisons, A. Malhotra.

[EDV] What are your thoughts on the national bookstore chains such as Crossword and Landmark which often find themselves in the (ever increasing) shopping malls across India – Bahrisons seems a world away from that sort of book commerce and culture, or is it?

[AB] In my opinion, these are not bookstores – they are merchandisers. They are there only to make money out of the retail space. These are retailers who are only interested in filling up the huge space that they are working in – while smaller bookshops are curators of collections and care about what you want to read and not what the publisher wants to display. Commerce is important, but not at the cost of your reputation. We are first booksellers and then business people.

[EDV] What do you mean by being 'a bookseller'? What kind of person is a 'book seller', how might you describe such?

[AB] Booksellers are curators of collections and care about what you want to read and cater to your needs in accordance. A bookseller is someone who likes to serve generations in a family because it is a relationship not of money or trade, but of intellect and reasoning. The money earned as a bookseller may not be the best, but I believe that the trust and the respect that you earn in society cannot be valued in money.

[EDV] As CEO of Bahrisons for 15 years now, what have been the most significant changes for you in terms of the post-liberalisation period? Has the manner in which you buy and sell books changed significantly or has the process remained the same? Could you also say a little about how Khan Market and the changes that it has seen post millennium might have impacted your business? Have there been any challenges that have proved difficult to overcome?

[AB] Fifteen years … post liberalisation … well, there is so much more to read and write about. As a bookseller, I love the new period of debate that we are passing through. There are so many new ways to look at an issue and the world is just about opening up for us, for India. I think bookselling is not too complicated a trade. The key is to know your customers and once you do that, the selection becomes easy. The means and mode of ordering may have changed over the years, but selections – how can that change? Your choice of books is an integral part of who you are. All booksellers build collections to suit the needs of its readers and our collection is who we are – it speaks of us as people and of our lives. At the end of the day it is still a business and all businesses have challenges so in that sense, we are no different from the rest of the world of business.

[EDV] Could you share a couple of examples of the challenges that you face in this New India?

[AB] Life has changed for the young and moves at a pace and that, I should say, I do not understand much. The New India is fast paced and is moving at a higher technological speed … maybe too fast for my liking, but that is life – live with it or get left out! The changing life patterns and lifestyles are not a problem in essence but maybe the speed at which life is changing might become a challenge one day!

[EDV] It was through an email communication with you a few years ago that I experienced my first 'book trailer', embedded as it was in your email signature at the time. Could you tell me about some of the marketing strategies at Bahrisons and how these might have changed over the last 15 years. What is your main medium for marketing new books and do you market all your titles or concentrate on fiction?

[AB] We carry all titles – all kinds of books. We are a retail 'bookstore' in the sense that we carry everything. There are many ways to market your products today, but when you are marketing other people's wares the only thing that places you apart from the rest, is your reputation. It matters who you are. It is the trust of the reader that brings them back to you for a consolidated stock of other books that you end up curating for your readers.

[EDV] This sounds as if you rely on a very core and loyal customer base – is this the case? If so, what about reaching out to potential, new customers?

[AB] I am a retailer – the old name for which is a 'shopkeeper' and the first thing that you learn as a shopkeeper is patience and relationship. The patience is about waiting and about building relations. Your relations and your good nature is what bring people back to you – these are the people who will see to your wellbeing and to your survival. The old saying in India is *grahak aur maut ka intezaar karna padta hai* – 'you always wait for your customer and for death – they won't come to you even if you stand outside and call them.'

[EDV] Since the early 2000s there has been a boom in popular paperbacks, often in English, authors such as Amish Tripathi, Anuja Chauhan, Ashwin Sanghi, Advaita Kala to name a few. How has this proliferation of popular fiction played out at Bahrisons?

[AB] We are still a conservative, serious sort of a bookstore, more political and current affairs, but like I said earlier – we are retailers and carry everything so popular fiction is part of our catalogue.

[EDV] I understand that you run Red Ink Literary Agency, could you say how this came about, what were the motivating factors to establish Red Ink and how does it run day-to-day? What are the challenges in running a literary agency – is the business of author representation a difficult one?

[AB] Yes, that was an addition to my life as a bookseller. It started with wanting to give an equal opportunity to all kinds of writing and to offer an even, international platform to such writing. Why should that unknown Indian not be able to present his writings to a world reader? The choice is unlimited, I believe that there only needs to be an opportunity and a platform … this year, through the Red Ink Agency, we are facilitating getting Stieg Larsson into Indian language editions and our own local PINJAR – Amrita Pritam – to a European audience.

[EDV] Please describe the Bahrisons of today in three words:

[AB] *kal, aaj aur kal* – 'yesterday, today and tomorrow'

'yesterday' is our heritage, 'today' is what we are as a culture, 'tomorrow' is who we will be as a race. I think that this is what a bookstore tells you – all under one roof!!

[EDV] Anuj Bahri – thank you for taking the time to engage with these questions.

Talking with the CEO of Bahrisons reveals that to remain competitive in New India is, for Bahrisons at least, a multifaceted endeavour. Whilst pursuing new business activity – such as the creation of the Red Ink Literary Agency – is an important element of maintaining a successful independent bookstore in post-millennial India, it is the reputation and the established, recognisable motifs of the 'Bahrisons experience' that speak of its continued success and patronage. Here we also learn that Anuj Bahri is quick to separate out 'bookshops' from what he calls 'merchandisers' such as national bookstores like Crossword and Landmark, and it is the quintessential customer experience of rummaging around for books at Bahrisons which is indicative in representing this difference.

Looking down towards the main entrance. Image © Bahrisons, A. Malhotra.

Following in the shop's tradition of making use of every available space, Bahrisons has recently 'expanded' (upwards) to include a new level of books, arranged floor to ceiling which is in keeping with the rest of the shop. The continual and indeed, expanding stock of books chart both the academic and the popular fiction interests of post-millennial India through their material presence as well as through the customers they attract.

Curiously, Bahrisons embodies both old and new India within its walls. The book trailers of the Red Ink agency travel far and wide via the company's emails whilst some of Bahrisons long-standing patrons need only take a short rickshaw ride to browse the new stock.

ORCID

E. Dawson Varughese http://orcid.org/0000-0001-6337-4462

Impacts of funding in digitising the Bangladesh film industry: Challenges ahead

Muhammad Shajjad Ahsan

ABSTRACT
Although the impacts of government funding in digitising the Bangladesh Film Industry is noticeable, the aspiration of growth to be expected has not yet been met. No studies were found to identify the reasons why the digitisation project took over a decade and failed to attain its goal satisfactorily. This paper therefore aims to explore the funding impacts by considering two issues: whether the project has enhanced or lessened the BFI's productivity and eventually widened or narrowed the market's business to business relationship within and beyond the stakeholders in the digital era. In-depth interviews of the industry professionals and secondary data sources were used for this study. Empirical results reveal that workforce derelictions in learning the digital technology and overarching business dominance of few stakeholders have a perceived impact on the productivity of the industry. This study therefore suggests that a desegregated and carefully balanced market policy would enable the government to tackle the challenges and create a positive impact of their funding.

1. Introduction

In 2003, when the Film Development Corporation (FDC) in Bangladesh took the initiative to revolutionise its celluloid-based production and printing facilities into the digital technology, this quick response was perceived as the 'early adoption' effort of this state-owned organisation towards the newly innovated technology. After more than a decade in June 2015, when the project was re-evaluated, it was noticed that the FDC had repeatedly failed to complete this project timely and attempted only 80% towards its completion. The reason for this part-fulfillment and fragmented progress of the project either could be the FDC's underperformance in procuring and disseminating the technology within its own organisation (production) or acclaiming the new technology within its business stakeholders (i.e. distributors and exhibitors). In this regard, it is crucial to understand whether the publicly funded project has created any impacts on the film industry, if at all.

Therefore, this paper is aiming to attain the following main objectives:

To briefly review some key indicators that will help us to understand the impacts of investments/funding such as (i) enhanced/lessened productivity, (ii) widened/narrowed market i.e. business to business (B2B) relationship within and beyond the stakeholders. This study will ascertain what the policies are which need to be addressed in basking accomplishments through defined utilisation of funding and investments for digital film production, distribution and exhibition.

2. Methods

This study has collected empirical data from the FDC and the Bangladesh Film Industry (BFI) professionals. The information required to understand a lot of the qualitative data in this research was acquired through face-to-face interviews with industry professionals such as high officials, executives, entrepreneurs and creative personnel. Information from online newspaper articles and respective websites was taken into consideration when conducting secondary sources for this research. Data collected during the previous fieldwork in 2008–2009 of the research were compared with recently visited data from 2014 to 2015 to understand the impacts of digitalisation within the FDC.

3. Current scenarios

Since 2012, when the Government of Bangladesh declared the film production, distribution and exhibition sectors as an 'industry', apart from the auditing, no policies have yet been devised to measure the industry's growth or impacts of the development projects. Although the office of the comptroller and auditor general (OCAG)'s auditing helped us to understand the financial irregularities during the FDC's digitisation project, no studies were found to comprehend the scenario of the post-digitisation phase.

In a recent study, Ahsan and Malik (151–156) documented the weaknesses of the FDC's procurement process which could be supportive in understanding the consequences of publicly funded project. In the study, it was detected that during the procurement, many non-functional, used and unrelated equipment were purchased which ultimately hampered the progress of the FDC's digitalisation. Apart from the empirical study, further testimony was found to understand the outgrowth stage of the digitalisation project. A news report disclosed that the first project director (PD) of the digitalisation project was sacked from his job due to allegations of malpractice in procurement (Correspondent). A face-to-face interview was recorded in the same year also echoed the same narratives (Ahsan, 138). A member of the FDC's technical committee for camera procurement unveiled his experience. He stated,

> The administration says that they are importing German-made cameras but in reality, they are actually importing Chinese ones. The most interesting thing is that after all these malpractices happening in Bangladesh, various investigations are taking place; but nothing is happening to FDC. (Batchu)

It was thought that after such a whistle-blowing situation at the beginning of the digitalisation project, the occurrence of financial irregularities would discontinue at later stage. In reality, it did not. However, in 2015, another news report uncovered that the Anti Corruption Bureau of Bangladesh had filed a charge against the current PD and three other high officials with the same accusation (Reporter). These explicit instances posit that continuous malpractice in procurement might have created an adverse impact in the progress and completion of the digitalisation.

In this vein, it is now crucial to know whether the procurement downfall has disrupted the film production or not.

Since the project's initiation in 2003, it took almost 4 years to motivate the FDC's private workforce to adopt the digital technology. *Captain Maruf* (2007) was the first film to be shot digitally for a FDC release. In 2009, when digital films were first allowed to be censored, the number of productions increased little by little and nowadays the majority of the FDC's films are being produced digitally.

Although it seems that the digitalisation project has a direct impact on producing the digital film, the industry's productivity growth is still not satisfactory.

The historical data shown on Table 1 indicate that the FDC released a maximum of 144 celluloid productions in 2006 ("List of Certified Bangla Films" 1–68). This statistics show that the FDC's productivity is still underperforming in the digital era. Since the start of digital technology integration in 2003, the FDC produced its highest number of films (88) in 2014. In the same year, the number of celluloid production turned to zero. The FDC's present productivity requires at least a growth of 130% to reach its previous celluloid productivity height.

The low return on investment was found to be the underlying reason of this low productivity. Lone producers are losing their businesses by competing against the corporate producers such as Jaaz Multimedia and Tiger Media. Many lone producers who are investing money to produce one (single) movie are facing low returns on their investments or a complete loss. For instance, anecdotal evidence was found during the recent data collection. One of the interviewee discloses the situation of his alleys,

> Although my alley's invested film won 'Best Actress Award' nationally, he could not offset his investment losses against his single screen release income. When his business fails, he then applied to the government to have a license for exporting Bangladesh films to India and importing Indian Films to Bangladesh for screenings. (Roy)

Since 2010 when the current Hasina government in Bangladesh lifted a four-decade ban on importing Indian films, a number of people engaged themselves to make some profit from this bilateral trade business ("Bangladesh Lifts Ban on Indian Films"). It was evident from the fieldwork that many sole producers were not able to cope up with the corporate producers. Therefore, many of them either quitting the business or losing their bravery to newly reinvest themselves in another venture.

The polar difference between the sole producer and corporate producer is not only limited to capital investment capacity or legal differences but also involvement and controls of film

Table 1. Celluloid and digital films released in the BFDC.

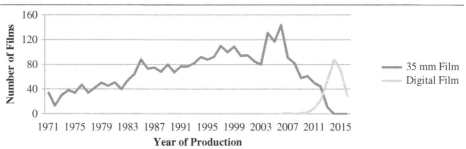

studio, distributing and exhibiting arms. Within the two major corporate film-producing companies the Jazz Multimedia has appeared in the Bangladesh Film Industry as an intermediary force. One of the film directors argued that due to the excessive profit-making attitudes of the intermediaries, the solo producers were unable to secure their return on investment. He explained,

> If in one cinema sells a total of BDT 200,000 the producer should preferably have BDT 100,000 as revenue. In reality, these days the producer only has BDT 30,000 to 40,000. The rest of the revenues are slashed by the intermediaries such as booking agent, producer's representative, and cinema hall management and server owners. (Guljar)

Traditionally, the 'celluloid film producers' never used to pay any extra money to the exhibitors other than a negotiated profit margin on ticket sales. Nowadays, intermediary force such as Jazz Multimedia are charging money from the 'digital film producers' to use their digital film projectors as the exhibitors do not have any digital screening facilities.

As the expenditure rose dramatically when many lone producers closed their businesses, many crews and staffs relied on the small firms and found themselves in a most awkward quandary and therefore some of them gave up their freelancing job and some began working under the corporate umbrella. As a result of that in the post-funding phase, a sharp decline of the number of the workforce in the BFI has been noticeable.

Previous research in the Bangladesh Film Industry (BFI) showed that the total number of their workforce was 7983 in 2012 (Ahsan 1–277). This figure has however recently been found to decrease down to 4645 (Ahsan and Dudrah 147–173). The Table 2 data reveal that the BFI has actually lost 41.75% of its previous workforce as an effect of its digitalisation. While searching the reason behind the job loss and voluntary redundancy, the qualitative data from several interviews disclosed that the FDC's lack of growing business-to-business (B2B) relationship within them was to blame. For example, while digitising the cinemas, Jazz Multimedia has appointed a trained operator to run their digital screening facility alone. This new workforce has instantly replaced the 2–3 35 mm projectionists who were working there. The cinema's owner did not take any initiative to retain his operator into the job by providing him the new skills (Mia).

Hence, it would not be illogical to predict that the actual job loss of the previous workforce could be higher than the data shown in Table 2. Moreover, many former workforces such as directors, editors or cameramen who were not trained with digital skills are currently

Table 2. Workforce tally of the Bangladesh Film Industry (Ahsan).

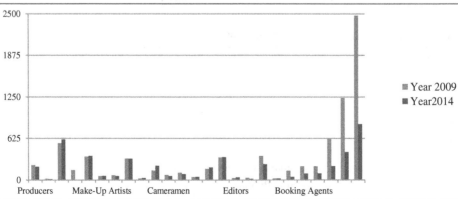

working with the digitally skilled new workface as their assistants or operators to complete their jobs. (Zahir).

Working on creative jobs in a double-layer sequence (cameramen-operator) is requiring more time and money. For instance, previously during the celluloid film era, while a film editor used to edit the full length feature film solely, nowadays a two member group can be seen carrying out the same job. It was evident from the digital editing suit that the film editor instructs the software operator to carry out the editing under his creative decisions. Neither the editor is able to operate the non-linear editing (NLE) suite by himself nor is the operator able to perform editing with their own creative initiative. Although it might be seen as an ice-breaking praxis between the old and new workforce, the adverse effect of it of reducing the productivity cannot be ignored. Creative jobs require many trial and errors until a solution is found. When a crew tries to solve a problem by thinking intensely about it, ideally they might not be able to instruct it to the operator instantly. As the operator is not able to take part in the brainstorming, any interruptions tend to obstruct the creativity, time and money.

During the digitisation phase, many exhibitors closed down their cinemas as they could not equip their halls with digital projection and sound systems due to the technological and financial incapability. Therefore, the data reveal that although in 2011 there were a total of 608 cinemas operating, now there are only 353 cinemas in operation ("Yearly Report 2015" 1–59).

Digital technology created an unprecedented change in the existing distribution system within the industry. In the film industry, manual distribution has existed for decades via the intermediaries such as the distributing arms and booking agents. It was speculated that soon after inaugurating digital technology, a server-based intranet system would emerge and the film content would reach from the producers to the exhibitors directly without any intermediaries. In reality, the legacies of the intermediaries are still very much active in the digital era and in addition a new intermediary force has entered the supply chain.

As the producer did not develop online distribution and the exhibitors did not transform their cinema halls with digital gadgets, a new mediator appeared in the market to rent out their gadgets to the exhibitors. This new entrant is not only earning rental revenues from the exhibitors for their machineries, but also charging fees from the producers to encode the film content into their server s to be screened. The new mediator's aggressive market penetration has rapidly changed the legacy of the B2B relationship. Nowadays, it is becoming challenging for the rest of the stakeholders such as individual producing firms, soul distributors or single exhibitors to understand and cope with new mediators such as Jazz Multimedia. Within the last couple of years, Jazz has equipped 130 cinemas with a digital screening set-up. The chairman of the Jazz Multimedia elaborated his business plan:

> We have a plan to convert an additional 120 cinemas with digital screening capacity by the next Eid (2016). Moreover we are trying to negotiate with the exhibitors to lease out another 250 already closed cinemas and reopen them for the audience. (Aziz)

If Jazz can transform and untie a total of 500 cinemas with digital screen, they will certainly appear as a major and powerful stakeholder in the market. Zhao et al. (383) claims that the 'appropriate use of power can significantly enhance relationship commitment'. Jazz's precedence as a booming stakeholder has inspired another India-based international distributing company,UFO, to establish their business in Bangladesh. They have already equipped 28 cinemas with digital screening facility and aim for a total of 250 cinemas to deal with (Dey, 2016). The Bangladesh Government is also aiming to convert a total of 64 cinemas or auditoriums in the 64 districts with digital screening capacity across the country (Mia, 2016). If all the planned 814 digital cinemas become operational, the film market will witness a new B2B relationship. The healthy partaking within the stakeholders might ensure the usual return of the investments and help the market to grow.

Yielding positive results in marketing is primarily reliant on the B2B relationship. Therefore, the following part will examine the B2B relationship between the FDC and its stakeholders to understand the impact of the investment. Apart from the procurement and production, the success of any investment is also dependent on effective marketing. It was revealed that prior to launching this project, no market study was conducted by FDC (Ghosh).

4. Discussion and recommendations

Measuring the impacts of government funding instantly is not often achievable in Bangladesh. It is most likely to expect that the managing director (MD) of the FDC would take care in ensuring the successful and well-timed completion of any ongoing projects. Data reveal that since the establishment of the FDC on the 1 December 1957 till now, the government has appointed 43 MD's to run the FDC. This means in the last 59 years, the average engagement period of an MD was only 16 months. Such a short period has appeared as a serious drawback for tracking and ensuring the completion of the digitalisation project. During the current project, the government has changed the FDC's MD 11 times. As a result, the project which was supposed to be completed in 3 years of inauguration is still yet to be completed in its 13th year. Therefore, logically, it should be suggested that the government should allow a particular person to run an organisation for the period of the completion of any running project.

This study therefore suggests that a full report, with the support of the internal and central audit report, should be made by every new MD about their previous MD when they are appointed their new position. Moreover, before they finish their own period in the position, current MDs should take it upon themselves to make a report of them to hand to the respective ministry. This report should include the impact measurements of any projects that have been completed in their tenure. As a lot of these projects are of a technical nature, appropriate university faculty scholars, researches and professionals should be carefully inducted to be part of this organisation. Qualitative indicators should particularly be emphasised on during these assessments to easily spot loopholes in the projects. Quantitative data usually involve a lot of mathematical modelling and financial jargon which is difficult to spot errors in from an outside point of view in the case of corruption and irregularities.

The necessity of improving a competitive film market is essential. The recent dominance of a particular intermediary force in the supply chain is suggesting that they might grow as a monopolistic force someday. If so, they might desire to have exclusive control over a commercial activity by possession or financial endowment. Therefore, in order to avoid such an uncompetitive business environment, the government should intervene and devise a policy to protect the small entrepreneurs. Moreover, boosting government funding in the distributing and exhibiting businesses will certainly facilitate the industry to grow coordinately, justly and uniformly.

A policy which will allow a balanced sharing of revenue among the stakeholders is crucial for the survival of the Bangladesh Film Industry. If the producers are unable to return their investment, the industry will suffer from financial crisis. Therefore, the trust and a harmonious arrangement or relation of the stakeholders within the whole industry is the key to the industry's subsistence. Moreover, vigilant attentiveness should be paid to ensure the applications of the existing national policies are also vital for guaranteeing a greater customer satisfaction. For example, one of the responded admitted that,

> The Bangladesh Film Censor Board asked the exhibitors to install a 2K resolution projector for the cinemas. As, this is really expensive to spend money between USD $30,000 to 70,000 without VAT therefore, in order to avoid the huge expenses they installed an inferior quality projector with 720 × 1200 pixel resolution. (Nabi)

According to the above stated interview it seems that many cinemas that were digitalised were in fact done unprofessionally and below the national standard i.e. 2K resolutions. Although no direct evidence was found to further prove this statement, it was palpable from the Jazz Multimedia's business policy of categorising their affiliated Cinema halls into A, B, C and D. These types of categorisation might be based on variations in image quality and geographical locations of the cinemas. Additionally, while looking into the government reports of the Bangladesh Film Censor Board (BFCB) no monitoring information was found to check the resolutions of the cinema halls projectors during their routine inspection. In 2013, the BFCB inspectors visited 189 cinemas and 23 prints were banned and withdrawn from screenings. No report was observable in ceasing inferior quality projectors from the operation.

Replacing the old workforce with the new workforce should be done gradually and unhurriedly. Since 1959, FDCs establishment was enriched over six decades through its many prodigiously talented workforces. Therefore, the wisdom, understanding, know-how of film-making that's the old worker have acquainted should not be ignored by the new workforce. The new workforce might learn from the struggles, patience and maturity of the old workers. Although the current trend of the double-layer workforce might appear as a threat of delayed output, the affiliation between the old and new workers might bring new dynamics in the filmmaking. Moreover, a lot of creativity might remain unexplored or unused due to misunderstanding or miscommunication between the two would play down. Therefore, one of the interviewees suggested that digitally training up the old workforce would allow them to fully use their potential (Zahir).

5. Conclusion

This study initially tried to observe the impacts of public funding on the FDC in Bangladesh. Out of many indicators, this study has narrowed down the key focus on two particular indicators: productivity growth, and business to business relations. This study found that the project was not completed in its proposed time frame. However, after its long delay, the FDC's traditional production capability has finally integrated into its digital upgrade, which has been the main goal for this industry since 2003. This longitudinal data indicated that there has been a sharp decline in the number of the workforce. The pace at which the FDC integrated them towards digital technology has not been carried out to the same level by the distributing and exhibiting firms of the industry. This study therefore suggested that addressing the existing challenges and devising a competitive B2B relationship, aiming a greater customer satisfaction and training up the workforce fully would be the key to enhance digital film productivity.

Disclosure statement

No potential conflict of interest was reported by the author.

References

AFP. "Bangladesh Lifts Ban on Indian Films." *Talkvietnam.com*. N.p. 24 Apr. 2010. Web. 23 Feb. 2017. <http://www.independent.co.uk/arts-entertainment/films/bangladeshlifts-ban-on-indian-films-5537220.html>.

Ahsan, Muhammad S. "Integration of Digital Technology in the Film Industry of Bangladesh: Readiness and Response Functions." Diss. Faculty of Humanities, University of Manchester, 2012.

Ahsan, Muhammad Shajjad. *Members List of the 26 Groups of Film Professionals (2008 and 2014)*. n.d. Workforce Tally of the Bangladesh Film Industry.

Ahsan Muhammad Shajjad, and Rajinder Dudrah. "Bangladesh Film Industry: Challenges and Opportunities of Workforce Development in the Digital Age." *The Jahangirnagar Review, Part-C* XXVI (2015): 147–173. Print.

Ahsan Muhammad Shajjad, and Khaleel Malik. "The Role of an Intermediary Agent in Technology Integration Within Developing Countries: A Film Industry Perspective." *Procedia-Social and Behavioral Sciences* 195 (2015): 151–156.

Aziz, Abdul. Personal interview. 15 May. 2016.

Batchu, Abdul. Personal interview. 12 May. 2008.

Captain Maruf. Dir. Kazi Hayat. Unilever. 2007. Film. <https://www.youtube.com/watch?v=ZYXdvdFc8QI>.

Correspondent, Staff. "The Project Director Will Be Sued FDC 3 ACC." *The Daily Nayadiganta* [Dhaka] 29 Aug. 2015: n.pag. Print.

Dey, Kartik. Personal interview. 12 May. 2016.

Ghosh, Tapan. Personal interview. 12 May. 2016.

Guljar, Mushfikur. Personal interview. 12 May. 2016.

Jackson Edward T. "Evaluating social impact bonds: questions, challenges, innovations, and possibilities in measuring outcomes in impact investing." *Community Development* 44(5) (2013): 608–616.

"List of Certified Bangla Films." Http://www.bfcb.gov.bd/. Bangladesh Film Censor Board, n.d. Web. 23 Feb. 2017.

Mia, Alauddin. Personal interview. 11 May. 2016.

Nabi, Nurun. Personal interview. 8 May. 2016.

Reporter, Senior. "Pijush Sued on Graft Charge." *Newsbangladesh.com* [Dhaka] 07 Oct. 2015: n. pag. Print.

Roy, Bibesh. Telephone interview. 1 Jul. 2016.

"Yearly Report 2015." *Bangladesh Film Censor Board*. N.p., n.d. Web. 22 Feb. 2017.

Zahir, Sajjad. Personal interview. 8 May. 2016.

Zhao Xiande, et al. "The impact of power and relationship commitment on the integration between manufacturers and customers in a supply chain." *Journal of Operations Management* 26 (2008): 368–388.

Creative enterprise from the medieval to the modern period: Alternative perspectives

Catherine Casson

ABSTRACT
Entrepreneurs have generated creative ideas for many centuries, and across a range of industries. Two books have recently appeared addressing the issue of entrepreneurial creativity from different perspectives. They are compared and contrasted in this article. Historical precedents for innovation are examined in one, while contemporary examples are the focus of Tsang's volume. Strategies used to encourage innovation in medieval and early modern towns inform on contemporary debates on the role of traditional industries in India. Experiments in new forms of production were encouraged, rather than deterred, and investment in training helped traditional crafts to retain a reputation for quality and develop regional specialisms. Both books highlight that necessity can encourage innovation, a situation which has parallels to current debates on frugal innovation in India.

Two books have recently appeared addressing the issue of entrepreneurial creativity from different perspectives. These two books are Tsang, *Entrepreneurial Creativity in a Virtual World* (Edward Elgar: Cheltenham) and Davids and de Munck, *Innovation and Creativity in Late Medieval and Early Modern European Cities* (Ashgate: Farnham) and they are compared and contrasted here.

Entrepreneurs have generated creative ideas for many centuries, and across a range of creative industries, as these two books show. Davids and de Munck's edited volume aims to identify the circumstances that encouraged innovation in medieval and early modern cities. They focus on 'why' innovation in the creative sector occurred at certain times and in certain places. Three key explanations are provided for this: 'Guilds and technological innovation', 'migration, citizenship and the spatial circulation of knowledge' and 'urban networks, urban hierarchies, state formation and centralization'. Tsang's book, meanwhile, focuses on 'how' innovation occurs, with a particular focus on product and content development. She investigates the contemporary industries of online magazines, gaming, and television in the UK. She argues that the effective management of people and production processes permits successful innovation.

Coordination is a key theme across both books. Entrepreneurs, in Tsang's view, are responsible for the effective coordination of complex creative processes that represent a 'synergy of traditional craftsmanship and modern marketing' (4). In the online magazine and gaming sectors, the entrepreneur is usually the founder or founders of the business; in the online television sector the producer of the show is often the individual who exhibits the characteristics of risk, innovation and judgement. Tsang emphasises, however, that entrepreneurs in these sectors need to provide a relatively informal management style that allows creativity to flourish while still ensuring a viable business.

Delegation is also an important characteristic of a successful entrepreneur when coordinating activities in the online creative industries. This can be delegation to colleagues and employees but also delegation to customers. In one of her case studies of an unnamed television comedy show, Tsang shows how the producer of the show allowed the actors both to contribute to the script-writing and to provide online personas for the characters on social media sites. The opportunity to receive status updates and Twitter feed from the actors 'in character' was seen as a key part of the show's success in attracting and retaining viewers. In the online magazine industries, content is often obtained from freelance writers as well as from permanently employed payroll staff. Tsang suggests that this is one of the more transitory relationships involving delegation. In the online gaming environment, the process of delegation usually involves outsourcing elements (such as animation) to specialist firms. In this instance the delegation can often involve a degree of embeddedness, as in some instances outsourced staff will work alongside core staff in the main company office.

Customers, Tsang suggests, can be delegated some responsibility for marketing products. This is particularly the case in the online gaming industry, where the 'pay for early access' model of game development has become increasingly popular. This model was initially intended to benefit firms by allowing them to raise extra capital for development and to spot any technical problems early. One of the unexpected additional benefits, however, was that 'pay for early access games' began to be marketed organically by their fans through online forums. The Angry Birds franchise of online games, meanwhile, intentionally encouraged customer-led marketing by posting clips on You Tube which fans could then share.

Coordination provided by trade organisations and location government institutions is the focus of the edited *Innovation and Creativity* volume. Trade organisations have often been viewed as having a detrimental impact on innovation by encouraging standardisation of techniques and products, rather than variation. Local government, meanwhile, has traditionally been considered to have deterred the spread of innovative ideas by discouraging migration and immigration. Overall, this volume takes a more positive approach to the role of trade organisations and local government. Many contributors suggest that this coordination aided innovation by allowing improved production and marketing techniques to be disseminated more rapidly. In Venetian glassmaking, for example, trade organisations encouraged innovation 'of new products that met the desire of the urban elite for 'refinement" (35). In an echo of Tsang's finding, customer-led innovation was also present in the glass sector. In the 1480s, customers from Germany asked Murano glassmakers to produce rods of glass, which were then pierced and strung into beads in Germany, before being exported to Venice and on to the eastern Mediterranean. This innovation was so popular that the Venetians decided in 1505 to officially recognise and legalise it in their guild statutes.

Local government's attitude to creative innovation seems to have varied between locations. In Venice, in particular the contribution of the glassmaking and soap production industries to the city's economy was recognised and the local government took a close interest in those sectors, even prohibiting skilled artisans from emigrating. In other locations, local government focused more on attracting immigrants in order to increase the skills base. This was a key strategy in eighteenth-century Trieste, which managed to transition from an 'imitation centre' to an 'innovation centre' through this policy (349). The royal porcelain factories of Naples, meanwhile, were established with a team of painters, modellers and miners from locations including Parma, Florence and Dresden. As the factories expanded, local Neapolitan talent began to be employed to a greater extent.

Entrepreneurship is a topic that would have benefitted from greater elaboration upon in *Innovation and Creativity*. While this does not purport to be the focus of the volume, the focus on institutions means that the topic is sometimes dismissed quite quickly when it appears. Demo's chapter on the silk industry of Vicenza mentions enterprising nobles who acquired new inventions from foreign countries for their subjects, but no further information on this process is provided. Likewise Andreozzi's paper on the development of a commercial manufacturing and craft sector in Trieste, and Ammannati's on Florentine wool production, also allude to attempts to attract entrepreneurs to the cities, and the importance of merchant capital investment. Again, however, the focus on institutions means that little additional information is provided.

A corresponding gap appears in Tsang's volume, which is again partly connected to the book's focus. Unlike Davids and de Munck Tsang does not examine the broader political environment within which the three creative industries operate. It might have been interesting to know, for example, if any government support was available to start-ups in these areas. The advances in new technology that have permitted the development of the online sectors are also not examined in detail. Detailed examination of the existing scholarship on the fields of entrepreneurship and the creative industries is provided however.

Location is a second key theme in both books. All the authors agree that clusters or 'hotbeds' of creative innovation develop, either due to the location of human resources or due to particularly favourable regulatory environments. Both books emphasise the important role that cities play as knowledge hubs. Tsang demonstrates that, in the UK, London is the key location for the online television and magazine industries. This finding corresponds with results from other studies and occurs, she suggests, from a combination of inspirational surroundings (in the form of architecture and access to art galleries) and a myriad of opportunities for informal social networking. However, the geography of the online gaming industry is much more varied, spreading across the south-east of England, the Midlands and Scotland. This may reflect findings in previous literature regarding the role of other regions in supplying 'complementary inputs (such as raw materials and production technologies)' (96). The significance of regional innovation would have benefitted from further elaboration in Tsang's volume.

Italy and the Low Countries are the focus of *Innovation and Creativity*. While both locations benefit from rich surviving sources of evidence for the medieval and early modern period, the omission of England from the Davids and de Munck volume is slightly surprising, given that it was highly urbanised with significant institutions during the period of study. When summarising the contents of the volume, the editors suggest that two distinctive locational patterns can be seen. In Italy they argue, there was little room for innovation in the hinterlands of cities. In the Low Countries, in contrast, there was a strong pattern of core creative cities with a network of smaller towns who were 'assigned a particular function in the network, for example as a supplier of a specific type of raw material' (28). While the books examine different locations, the clustering of the publishing industry which Tsang commented upon in relation to online magazines also features in Rasterhoff's chapter on publishing in the Dutch Republic. Rasterhoff suggests that publishers were attracted by the characteristics of 'commerce in Amsterdam, academic life in Leiden and politics in the Hague' (173–4). As the export of books became important, the port of Rotterdam also entered onto this list. It would have been interesting to have seen these influences on clustering explored a little more in Tsang's discussion. Overall, while the findings from *Innovation to Creativity* have parallels to city and region pattern alluded to in Tsang, there remain unanswered questions across both books about what causes the imbalance between cities and regions.

Training and education is a theme that features prominently in *Innovation and Creativity*. It is also of contemporary relevance as debates revolve around the employment prospects of university graduates. In the glass, soap and textile industries there was a reluctance to change the traditional systems of training, and skills were generally learnt on the shop floor. In the Antwerp diamond market of the sixteenth and seventeenth centuries and the Antwerp art market of the late seventeenth and eighteenth centuries, however, new forms of training were seen as a solution to economic decline. In the Antwerp diamond market this involved narrowing the remit of training to focus on a specific cut, the Antwerp rose. This cut was considered to provide Antwerp with a competitive advantage over other locations during a period when it faced a contraction in the supply of the bigger and better diamonds. While initially a very successful solution, training provision was allowed to grow beyond the demand for the product, resulting in high unemployment rates in the industry. However, by the late seventeenth century the benefits of acquiring transferrable skills were beginning to be recognised. In a bid to stem a similar 'one size fits all' model of training that had developed in the Antwerp art market, a leading Antwerp artist proposed the establishment of an Art Academy. Alongside access to manual training in a workshop, students also received lessons in drawing from plaster casts and nude models, 'classes on perspective, geometry and anatomy, and lectures on art theory and mythology' (299). Not only did individual students benefit but, it was hoped, the Academy would create a 'ripple' effect in the regional economy (305) by attracting more wealthy patrons to the area (to purchase works) and by providing design skills to complement the practical craft training of guild apprenticeships in other sectors. While the Academy faced some challenges in the early years, its blended model of practical and formal education made individual students more economically competitive and increased international exports.

Enthusiasm appears to be the most desirable aspect for potential entrants into the online gaming and television sectors in particular. The lead founders of the gaming companies that Tsang examines had played computer games from childhood and also had strong interests in related areas such as music and travel. They later built upon this spark of enthusiasm with 'formal education in games-related disciplines' (such as physics, computing, music and animation) or 'on-the-job-training' (63). In Tsang's case study relating to the development of a television programme a mix of enthusiasm, strengthened by formal training and experience, was also present. The ideas that led to the script came from the university and first-job experiences of the two writers. The script was written with two particular comedy actors in mind and those actors possessed the ability for 'improvisation based on their experiences with live audiences' (31). The addition of a well-respected and experienced producer meant that 'commercial reality' and 'fun' could be combined successfully (31).

New and creative ideas can emerge out of both opportunity and necessity, both books suggest. One of the case studies in Tsang's book describes the development of a prison simulation computer game, which was inspired by three opportunities: A growing market for simulation games, the inclusion of a prison as an element within another game the case-study's company were making and, finally, the creative director's visit to Alcatraz prison during a holiday in San Francisco. The result was that the prison element was removed from the other game the company was creating and developed as a stand-alone project. In that instance, the opportunity led to the new and creative idea. In contrast, the Angry Birds computer game was developed as a 'planned strategy ... to create a valuable asset' and designed to have a 'simple user interface' (110–1). The initial success was then developed into a franchise, with spin-off games that introduced new characters and the development of a feature film. The difficulty with the Angry Birds strategy, which Tsang alludes to, is that the need to maximise the asset resulted in an over-exposure that eventually caused consumers to tire of the product and switch to other games.

Opportunity and necessity also feature as motivations for innovation in medieval and early modern Italy and the Low Countries. In the soap making industry in northern Italy, crises in the economy often encouraged artisans to experiment with new forms of production. Necessity also drove product innovation in woollen production in Florence in the fifteenth and sixteenth centuries. In response to increased competition in the luxury end of the market, Florentine weavers extended the range of cloth they produced both in breadth and depth. Production of a new range of 'second rate' cloth was authorised, which used a wider range of raw materials than the traditional luxury cloth, but was still of a high quality and became a popular item in both Florence and as an export good. These examples suggest that medieval and early modern trade organisations were more versatile, and responsive to economic challenges, than they are often perceived to be. Furthermore, there are examples of innovations introduced in response to opportunities. The establishment of porcelain factories in Naples in the eighteenth century was inspired by a desire to 'emulate the characteristics of Eastern products in an attempt ... to reproduce Chinese hard-paste porcelain' (315).

Readers of this journal will be interested in how these themes in these books can be researched in a South Asian context. The concept of creativity emerging out of necessity resonates with current research on frugal innovation in India. Work by Radjou and Prabhu (2015), among others, has shown that limited access to capital may often encourage, rather than deter, experiments in the adaption and creation of products. Both books showcase further examples of this. Firstly, the use of social media for marketing purposes, as discussed by Tsang, is a cost-effective way for a small company to promote goods or services. It also has the benefit of engaging consumers directly with the product – a cheaper way of acquiring information on their preferences compared to a formal R and D department. Secondly, the creation of new products from existing inventory and skills, as the soap-makers and weavers did, is a more economical option for an entrepreneur than acquiring additional materials or staff. The activities of the medieval guilds can be seen as earlier versions of contemporary energy-saving adaptations made to fridges and the energy-creating adaptions made to bicycles.

The question of how traditional industries can remain economically viable is of increasing interest in a South Asian context. In recent months, independent Indian jewellery businesses have faced competition from overseas markets and from branded jewellery (Pattanayak). Dubai has become a new focus for diamond cutting and polishing, a development that threatens diamond cutting and polishing factories operating in India. Consumers, meanwhile, are showing an increased preference for branded jewellery. Debate exists around the solution to these threats. While the Indian government is proposing improvements in hallmarking, independent jewellers are requesting government subsidies to prevent the migration of skilled diamond cutters into alternative jobs (Mishra). The analysis of Antwerp presented in the *Innovation and Creativity* volume suggests that the jewellers are right to be concerned about the impact of a skills-drain on their sector. However, the Antwerp example also suggests an alternative solution, namely greater investment in training and design to enable independent Indian jewellers to create a distinctive identity for their products.

In conclusion, both these books make a strong contribution to the field of innovation and creativity. While not directly covering the area of South Asia, both books address themes that appear in current research on innovation in a South Asian context. Tsang's book is likely to be of more direct interest to readers of this journal as she suggests that the future for the virtual world lies in closer collaboration between the UK and Asia. She also suggests that growing economies are recognising the economic importance of the creative industries with, for example, the Chinese government planning 'to double the contribution of creative industries to 5% of China's GDP by 2016' (46). *Innovation and Creativity* is primarily aimed at historians who are seeking to engage more with innovation policy, with chapters being rich in detail but sometimes leaving the broader implications of the findings to the reader. As the discussion above has shown, however, many of the themes discussed in the volume have a contemporary relevance. The particular value of *Innovation and Creativity* is, therefore, that it highlights the potential for more longitudinal research in this field.

Disclosure statement

No potential conflict of interest was reported by the author.

References

Davids, Karel, and Bert de Munck, eds. *Innovation and Creativity in Late Medieval and Early Modern European Cities*. Farnham: Ashgate, 2014. Print.
Mishra, Lalatendu. "The Gem and Jewellery Industry Asks for Government Help." *The Hindu*. 19 Jan. 2016. Web. 14 Apr. 2016. <http://www.thehindu.com/news/cities/mumbai/business/the-gem-jewellery-industry-asks-for-govt-help/article8122840.ece>.
Pattanayak, Banikinkar. "The Chain Effect: Organised Jewellery Market Shines Bright." *The Financial Express*. 15 Mar. 2015. Web. 14 Apr. 2016. <http://www.financialexpress.com/article/markets/commodities/the-chain-effect-organised-jewellery-market-shines-bright/53814/>.
Radjou, Navi, and Jaideep Prabhu. *Frugal Innovation: How To Do More With Less*. London: Profile Books, 2015. Print.
Tsang, Denise. *Entrepreneurial Creativity in a Virtual World*. Cheltenham: Edward Elgar, 2015. Print.

Index

Note: Page numbers in *italic* type refer to figures; Page numbers in **bold** type refer to tables; Page numbers followed by 'n' refer to notes

Abdin, R. 7
Adarsh, T. 45
AdiTi 24
Adorno, T. 83
advertised modernization 52
Agneepath (2012) 39
Agrawal, A. 36
Ahmedabad 78
Ahsan, M. S. 3, 106
Akhon: Where is Bengal Now 7, 15, 16
Alpay Er, H. 68
Angry Birds computer game 117
Anjum, M. 1, 7
Anti Corruption Bureau of Bangladesh 106
Antwerp diamond market 116
Arthur Andersen (AA), multinational accounting firm 84
'The Arts Britain Ignores' 23
Arts Council 'National Portfolio Organisations' 25
Arts Council's Ethnic Minorities Action Plan 23
Athique, A. 46n2
authorised heritage discourse (AHD) 25

Bahri, A. 100, 103
Bahrisons 3, 99–104
Banerjee, D. 57, 61
Bangalore 76–77
Bangladesh Film Censor Board (BFCB) 111
Bangladesh Film Development Corporation 3
Bangladesh film industry: business to business (B2B) relationship 106, 109, 110; current scenarios 106–110; digitising, funding impacts 105–111; Film Development Corporation (FDC) 105–107, 110, 111; methods 106
Bangladeshi creative industries, collaborative economy of 5–19
Bangladeshis, in Britain 5–139
Barry, N. 37–40
Basu, A. 52

Begum, L. 1
Behl, K. 61
Belgrade International Film Festival 60
Bengali 19n3; traditions 7
Berrey, E. 29
Bharatanatyam 24
Bharatiya Vidhya Bhavan, London 24
The Birth of the Clinic 38
BME engagement 29
Bodyguard (2011) 39
Bollywood film 33–48
Bollywood Hungama 45
Bolton, S. 3
Bonsiepe, G. 68
booksellers 102
Bordwell, D. 51
Bose, D. 53
Bowe, H. 45
Britain: South Asian arts in 22–31; South Asian arts organisations in 24–25
British Bangladeshi diaspora 2

Captain Maruf (2007) 106
Casson, C. 3, 4
celluloid films *107*
Charity Commission 17
Chaudhuri, S. 35
Chennai Express (2013) 53
Choi, Y. 67
Chopra, A. 33
Chopra, A. 45
Chopra, Y. 43
cinema 90; effect 52
Clarke, D. 25, 27, 28
Cleary, D. 44
The Closer You Get (2000) 45
clusters, defined 19n4
collaborative economy 9, 17, 18
communication failures 69
'community facing' organisations 25, 26, 29

competitiveness: design as tool 69–71; designing policy 67–69
compound annual growth rate (CAGR) 88, 96
Confederation of Indian Industry 69, 72, 74
Connolly, M. 41
Co-optex 74
Corbin, A. 36
country of origin principles programme 75
Cox report 64
craft industries 65
creative city, proponents 8
creative class 8, 9
creative cluster 8–9; in cultural policy-making 9
creative community 15
creative economy (CE) 19n1, 66
creative enterprise 113–118
creative industries (CI) 65, 66–67, 71, 84
creativity 1
Creswell, J. W. 34
Crossick, G. 22
crowdfunding 17
cultural pluralism 73
cultural value 22–23
Cunningham, S. 84

data collection: literature search 23; netnographic approach 7
data visualization 93
David, A. 28
Davids, K. 3, 113, 115
Dawson, K. 74, 75
DCMS 2016 report 19n1
Degun, J. S. 31n16
delegation 114
Delhi 77
de Munck, B. 3, 113, 115
Department of Culture, Media and Sport (DCMS) 66
De Propris, L. 8
Derby Caribbean Carnival 26
Desai, J. 36
Design Clinic Scheme (DCS) 71, 78
design/creativity theories 65
design hubs 77
design optimization 75–79; design, ISMEs 79; design education and skills 78; Indian SMEs 75–76; practices and applications 78–79; regional culture(s) and traditions 75–76; traditional and contemporary manufacturing 78–79; urbanisation, design ecosystems 76–78; visions and expectations, misalignment 78
design performance: culture and identity on 73–75; opportunities and challenges 71–73
design promotion 67–69
Dev D (2009) 59
Dharmic religions 73

diasporas 1, 46n3
digital films *107*
digital technology 109
digitisation 109
Dil Chahta Hai 36
Dilwale Dulhania Le Jayenge 36
'diversity' agenda 25
Doshi, S. 54
Dutta, P. 75

economic growth 1
economic liberalization 37, 84
economic value 26
Educating Rita (1983) 43
education 28
educational failures 69
Ek Tha Tiger (2012) 2; advertising Ireland 39–42; Hindi films and non-Indian locations 34–38; methodology 34; mutually beneficial relationship 34–38; production of 33–48; promotional vehicle 39–42; reception, Dublin and worldwide 44–45; stakeholders relevance, production 38–39; Trinity College Dublin, promoting 42–43
entrepreneurial creativity 113
Entrepreneurial Creativity in a Virtual World 3, 4
entrepreneurial endeavours 13
entrepreneurs 113
enumeration 83, 86–92
Equality Act 2010 23
Espeland, W. 93
'ethnic minority arts' 23–24
Evans, M. 67
exoticisation 34, 35
exoticism 34, 35

Far and Away (1992) 41
Farrell, G. 24, 28
Federation of Indian Chambers of Commerce and Industry (FICCI) 84, 86–88
FICCI-Arthur Andersen report 92
Film Censorship 91
Filmland 91
financial fact, visualization 92–97
financialization 83–97
Flew, T. 84
Florida, L. R. 1, 8
foreign investment 77
Foucault, M. 33, 35, 38
Freeman's stakeholder theory 34
Fringe Cinema 59

Ganti, T. 53, 91
Gibbons, L. 37
Gibbons, N. 40
Ging, D. 37, 45

INDEX

global media conglomeration 60
Goenka, G. P. 88
Goswami, A. 2
Govil, N. 3
Grainge, P. 52
Green, L. 3
Grimaud, E. 34
A Growth Story Unfolds report 86

Hansa (2012) 55
Hansen, T. B. 85
Hashmi, S. 27
heritage *see* Oitij-jo
Heskett, J. 67
Hickman, M. J. 41
Hidesign 75, 76
Hindie films 58
Hindustan Times 45
Hingorani, D. 27
Hirlekar, K. S. 90
Hodgson, T. 25, 27, 28
Hodgson, T. E. 30n3
Hollinshead, K. 35
Hoque, E. 7
Hylton, R. 23
Hypponen, L. 8

independent cinema 58–59
independent films 55
India Design Mark 71, 80n2
Indian Cinematographic Committee 91
Indian Entertainment and Media Outlook 94
Indian entertainment industry reports 83–97
Indian National Skill Development Corporation 67
Indian SMEs (ISMEs) 64–81
India Report 69
Innovation and Creativity in Late Medieval and Early Modern European Cities 4, 113–116, 118
innovation performance 64–81; creative industries and 66–67; culture and identity on 73–75
innovation policies 67
'Intelligent Rebellion: Women Artists of Pakistan exhibition' 27
In the Interval, but Ready for the Next Act report 86, 96
Ireland 33–48
Irish film 33–48
Irish Film Board 38
Irish Taxes Consolidation Act 37
Irish Tourism Board 39

Jaipur 78
Javid, S. 22
Jazz Multimedia 108, 109
Jedi Library 43

Joseph, M. 86
Jugaad 9

Kabul Express (2006) 44
Kadam 24
Kal Ho Naa Ho 36
Kapoor, A. 54
Kapoor, S. R. 55, 57
Kapuria, D. 76
Kashyap, A. 59
Kaszynska, P. 22
Kathak 24
Katrak, K. 31n14
Kaul, M. 55
Kaur, R. 46n3, 85
Khan, A. 54
Khan, K. 33, 37, 39, 43
Khan, N. 23, 24
Khan, S. 35, 45
Khan, S. R. 54
Khan Market 3; commerce and creativity 99–104
Khanna, A. 90, 95
Klynveld Peat Marwick Goerdeler (KPMG) 87
Koechlin, K. 58
Korean Institute of Design Promotion 72, 74
Kothari, B. 3
Kurbaan (2009) 53

Larsen, J. 41
Latour, B. 93
leadership qualities 1
Leicester Belgrave Mela 26
Lim, S. 67
literature search 23
Ludo (2015) 60
Lundvall, B. Å. 66

Maguire, P. J. 69
Malik, K. 106
Malik, S. 23
Margarita with a Straw 58
Marghi 24; traditions 28
marriage, of convenience 33–48
Marsh, M. 39
McAlex, A. 58
McDonald, P. 52
medical gaze 33, 40
Mehta, D. 35
Michael Collins (1996) 43
micro, small and medium enterprises (MSMEs) 71, 76, 78
Mijarul, Q. M. 7
Mommaas, H. 9
Mondal, A. 75
Monsoon Wedding (2001) 46n2

Mukherjee, Q. 60
Mumbai 77, 78
Mumbai Academy of Moving Image (MAMI) Film Festival 60

Nagle, D. J. 27
Nair, M. 46n2
national technology 67
New Bollywood: independent cinema and 58–59; marketing and exhibition, films 53–55; moment 51–53; *Phantomization* and 59–60; portfolio approach in 56–58
New Delhi 78, 99–104
New Hollywood 52
New-Wave cinema 58
New York (2009) 44
Non-Resident Indian (NRI) 52

Odissi 24
Oitij-jo 2, 5–19; collaborations, timeline *12*; creative class and clustering 8–9; digital and non-digital skills sharing map *11*; entrepreneurship 10–14; Facebook page 14; methodology 7–8; networks *13*; next steps 15–19; peer-to-peer skills sharing 10–14; steering committee 7; story of *10*; visualising, 'Past, Present, Future' 9–10
Olhmeyer, J. 43
Openvizor 7
ownership 14

Paan Singh Tomar (2010) 53
Pal, N. 91
Panesar, A. 39, 44
'parallel cinema' movement 58
Pettitt, L. 37
Phantomization 59–60
Place of Film in National Planning 90
Poovaya-Smith, N. 27
Porter, M. 9, 19n4
Prabhu, J. 117
Pratt, C. A. 8
Prickett, S. 27
product innovation 72–73
production house culture 51–62
'public facing' organisations 25, 29, 30n7
public funding 17
Punathambekar, A. 53, 87
Pune 77

Qureshi, I. 36

Radjou, N. 117
Rai, A. S. 52
Rajadhyaksha, A. 52
Rajput, J. 75, 78
Rampazzo, G. 2

Red Ink Literary Agency 103
Reshammiya, H. 47n26
Richard, S. 1
Robinson, M. 39
Rowdy Rathore (2012) 39

Sangam 34
SASIAN Journey platform 17
school curricula 27
self-reliant socialism 76
Shooting for the Stars **89**
Shorey, R. *35*
Singh, J. 2
Sinha, A. 55
'Size Matters' 92
small budget films 57
SME front-end innovation activities *70*
social integration 19
social media 4, 14
societal value 27–28
South Asian arts: in Britain 22–31; economic value 26; education 28; 'ethnic minority arts' 23–24; health and well-being 26; societal value 27–28; typology of 24
Staiger, J. 51
stardom 55–56
Star Wars Episode II (2002) 43
stereotypes 41
strategic leadership support 2
Strategy and Vision report 86, *89*
Sustaining Growth report 86
Syson, F. 28

technology, talent and tolerance (3Ts) 8
technology-stagnation 71
Temple Bar Trading Company 41
Teraa Surroor 47n26
textiles 74
Thompson, K. 51
3 Idiots (2009) 45
Throsby, D. 67
Tourism Ireland 38, 40, 42
tourist gaze 33–36
tourist industries 33–48
Travelling through Cinema Space (2014) 36
Trinity College Dublin 34, 42–43
Tsang, D. 3, 114, 116

An Unfolding Opportunity report 86, *93*, *96*
United Nations Conference on Trade and Development (UNCTAD) 8, 67, 68
Unraveling the Potential report 86, *94*
urban regeneration 1
Urry, J. 35, 40, 41

value agenda 23
Varadkar, L. 42, 47n3

Varughese, E. 3
Venetian glassmaking 113, 114
visualization, growth 85
Visvesvaraya, M. 91
Voluntary Arts England 26
volunteer feedback 15

Waking Ned (1999) 45
Wasko, J. 52
water (2005) 35
Waters, O. 42, 44
well-being 26

West Bengal 15
Wood, H. 28
Woodham, J. M. 69
work–life relationships 1
World Economic Forum Competitiveness index 67

Xerox policy 8

Yash Raj Films 33, 34, 36, 39, 42, 43

Zhao, X. 109